Advanced Spanish Vocabulary

Second Edition

Isabel Melero Orta

First published in 1995 by:
Mary Glasgow Publications, an imprint of Stanley Thornes (Publishers) Ltd

Second edition published in 2001 by:
Nelson Thornes Ltd
Delta Place
27 Bath Road
CHELTENHAM
GL53 7TH
United Kingdom

02 03 04 05 06 / 10 9 8 7 6 5 4 3 2

A catalogue record for this book is available from the British Library

ISBN 0 7487 5779 1

Typeset by Tech Set Ltd, Gateshead, Tyne and Wear
Printed in Croatia by Zrinski

ÍNDICE

INTRODUCCIÓN

Este libro ha sido escrito para ayudarte a adquirir el vocabulario que necesitas en temas que van desde la literatura hasta el medio ambiente.

Las palabras y las frases que contiene han sido clasificadas por temas, de forma que te puedan ser de utilidad para realizar composiciones orales o escritas, o bien como medio de repaso antes de un examen.

Sus quince capítulos tratan de temas de actualidad en España y contienen vocabulario y frases que reflejan los últimos cambios en el uso de la lengua.

En general no van incluidas las formas femeninas de las ocupaciones que se forman de una manera regular, p.ej., *enfermero – enfermera, vendedor – vendedora, capitán – capitana,* ni las que tienen la misma forma que la masculina, p.ej., *artista, representante.*

A través de la sección *Cómo ampliar tu vocabulario* aprenderás nuevas estrategias para memorizar palabras y frases. Elabora tu propio cuaderno de vocabulario donde puedas ir recopilando las palabras y expresiones que vayas aprendiendo. ¡Y no te olvides de utilizar un buen diccionario!

¡Buena suerte y diviértete!

Abreviaturas:

adv	adverb	*approx*	approximately	*coll*	colloquial
ej:	ejemplo	*euph*	euphemism	*f*	feminine
fig	figurative	*inf*	informal	*p.ej.*	por ejemplo
sl	slang				

Al final de cada sección, encontrarás una lista de direcciones útiles en internet, que te ayudarán a obtener más información sobre un tema que te interese. También puedes utilizar los motores de búsqueda siguientes:

www.yahoo.es
www.wanadoo.es
www.hispavista.com
www.biwe.es
www.metabusca.com
www.terra.es
www.altavista.es

LA GENTE

LA PAREJA

abandonar *to abandon*
el adulterio *adultery*
el afecto *affection*
la agencia matrimonial *dating agency*
el ama de casa (*f*) *housewife*
el amo de casa *house husband*
el amante *lover*
el amor *love*
la anticoncepción *contraception*
el banco de esperma *sperm bank*
la bigamia *bigamy*
bisexual *bisexual*
la boda *wedding*
el cariño *affection*
casarse (con) *to get married (to)*
la cita a ciegas *blind date*
cohabitar *to live together*
el compañero *partner*
la comprensión *understanding*
comprometerse *to get engaged*
la confianza *trust*
confiar (en alguien) *to trust (someone)*
el conflicto *conflict*
convivir *to live together*
la discusión *argument*
el divorcio *divorce*
la edad de consentimiento *age of consent*
enamorarse *to fall in love*
estar/ser celoso *to be jealous/to be a jealous person*
estar comprometido *to be engaged*
la fidelidad *faithfulness*
la franqueza *openness*
heterosexual *heterosexual*
homosexual *homosexual*
la honestidad *honesty*
la incompatibilidad *incompatibility*
la infidelidad *infidelity*
las labores del hogar *housework*
lesbiana *lesbian*
el ligue (*inf*) *boy/girlfriend*
la madrina *bridesmaid*
el matrimonio *marriage*
la monogamia *monogamy*
el novio/la novia *boyfriend/girlfriend*
la orientación matrimonial *marriage guidance*
el padrino *best man*
la pareja *partner/couple*
la pareja de hecho *unmarried couple (heterosexual or homosexual)*
la planificación familiar *family planning*
la relación *relationship*
la relación sexual *sexual intercourse*

el respeto *respect*
el sentimiento *feeling*
la separación *separation*
separarse *to separate*
ser fiel/infiel *to be faithful/unfaithful*
sexista *sexist*
soltero *single person*
el suegro/la suegra *father/mother-in-law*
las tareas domésticas *housework*
la tolerancia *tolerance*
la vida en común/conyugal *partnership*
vivir juntos *to live together*

la vida sexual	*sex life*
las citas por ordenador	*computer-dating*
recibir apoyo del/de la compañero/a	*to get support from one's partner*
solicitar un divorcio	*to sue for divorce*
abandonar a tu pareja	*to leave your partner*
usar anticonceptivos	*to use contraceptives*
incompatibilidad de caracteres	*mutual incompatibility*
la custodia de los hijos	*custody of the children*
obtener el divorcio	*to get divorced*
cometer adulterio	*to commit adultery*
tener una aventura amorosa	*to have an affair*
inseminación artificial	*artificial insemination*
irse a vivir juntos	*to move in together*
prueba de paternidad	*paternity test*
una relación platónica	*platonic relationship*
la ruptura matrimonial	*marriage break-up*

La Mujer

la baja maternal *maternity leave*
dar a luz *to give birth*
los derechos de la mujer *women's rights*
la discriminación sexual *sexual discrimination*
la emancipación de la mujer *emancipation of women*
el embarazo *pregnancy*
la esterilidad *infertility*
exitoso *successful*
la feminidad *femininity*
el feminismo *feminism*
el/la feminista *feminist*

la guardería *crèche*
la igualdad *equality*
la independencia *independence*
liberado *liberated*
el machismo *male chauvinism*
los malos tratos (a la mujer) *wife battering*
maternal *motherly*
la maternidad *motherhood*
la menopausia *menopause*
el movimiento feminista *feminist movement*
la ovulación *ovulation*
el parto *childbirth*
el período *period*
el prejuicio *prejudice*
la reafirmación *reaffirmation*
realizarse *to fulfil oneself*
la residencia para mujeres maltratadas *refuge for battered women*
la sala de partos *maternity ward*
los servicios de asistencia al niño *childcare services*
tomar la píldora *to be on the pill*
el vestido premamá *maternity dress*
volver al trabajo *to return to a career*

un embarazo (no) deseado	*a wanted (unwanted) pregnancy*
perder tu virginidad	*to lose your virginity*
el acoso sexual	*sexual harassment*
compartir las tareas del hogar	*to share the household jobs*
ser tratada como ciudadano de segunda clase	*to be treated as a second-class citizen*
la igualdad de oportunidades	*equal opportunities*
tener acceso a una vida profesional	*to have access to a career*
el reloj biológico	*biological clock*
estar dedicada a su profesión	*to be career oriented*

La Juventud

el aburrimiento *boredom*
la adolescencia *adolescence*
la agresividad *aggressiveness*
la amistad *friendship*
el argot callejero *street slang*
la autoridad paternal *paternal authority*
la autosuficiencia *self-sufficiency*
la banda callejera *street gang*
la barrera generacional *generation gap*
el club juvenil *youth club*
el complejo *complex*

el comportamiento	*behaviour*
el concierto de rock	*rock concert*
el conflicto generacional	*generation conflict*
crecer	*to grow up*
la delincuencia juvenil	*juvenile delinquency*
el delincuente juvenil	*juvenile delinquent*
deprimirse	*to get depressed*
el equipo juvenil	*youth team*
la escala de valores	*scale of values*
escandaloso	*outrageous*
escaparse de casa	*to run away from home*
estar de moda/pasado de moda	*to be fashionable/unfashionable*
idealista	*idealist*
el ídolo	*idol*
la incomprensión	*lack of understanding*
la independencia	*independence*
independizarse	*to become independent*
identificarse con	*to identify with*
la inseguridad	*insecurity*
llevarse bien/mal con	*to get on well/badly with*
la pandilla	*gang*
el pandillero	*member of a gang*
la pelea	*fight*
el piercing	*body piercing*
la pubertad	*puberty*
rebelarse (contra)	*to rebel (against)*
reñir	*to quarrel*
la sed de aventura	*thirst for adventure*
sentirse inseguro	*to feel insecure*
sobreproteger	*to overprotect*
el tatuaje	*tatoo*
el tribunal de menores	*juvenile court*
la tribu urbana	*urban tribe*
los valores familiares	*family values*
vulnerable	*vulnerable*

ser un miembro de la tribu	*to be a member of the tribe*
la falta de respeto a los demás	*lack of respect for others*
los jóvenes desocupados	*young people with nothing to do*
el problema de la delincuencia juvenil	*the problem of juvenile delinquency*
el desarrollo de la personalidad	*development of the personality*
querer independizarse	*to want one's independence*
las nuevas generaciones	*the rising generations*
dejar el hogar	*to leave home*
estar hecho un lío	*to be all mixed up*
questionarlo todo	*to question everything*

Los Derechos y Responsabilidades de los Jóvenes

el ciudadano *citizen*
crecer *to grow up*
el deber *duty*
el derecho al voto *the right to vote*
los derechos *rights*
egocéntrico *self-centred*
infantil *childish*
la ley de protección al menor *child-protection law*
la madurez *maturity*
maduro *mature*
la mayoría de edad *adult age*
la moralidad *morality*
el permiso de conducir *driving licence*
la responsabilidad *responsibility*
ser menor *to be under 18*
el tutor legal *legal guardian*

el sentido del deber *the sense of duty*
la libertad personal *personal freedom*
tener éxito en la vida *to succeed in life*
asumir las responsabilidades de uno *to take on one's responsibilities*
la autorización de los padres *parental consent*
ser responsable ante la ley *to be legally responsible*
actuar de forma irresponsable *to act irresponsibly*
llegar a la mayoría de edad *to come of age*
tolerar a los demás *to tolerate others*

La Vejez

el achaque *infirmity*
ágil *agile*
el anciano *old person*
el asilo de ancianos *old people's home*
delicado *delicate*
la demencia senil *senile dementia*
depender (de alguien) *to depend (on someone)*
dependiente *dependent*
la dignidad humana *human dignity*
duro de oído *hard of hearing*
el/la enfermero/a geriátrico/a *geriatric nurse*
envejecer *to get old*
la eutanasia *euthanasia*
el familiar *relative*
frágil *fragile*
el/la geriatra *geriatrician*

la geriatría *geriatrics*
la jubilación *pension*
la jubilación anticipada *early retirement*
el jubilado *retired person*
jubilarse *to retire*
los mayores *the old*
el/la pariente *relative*
la pensión de jubilación *old-age pension*
el/la pensionista *pensioner*
el plan de jubilación *pension scheme*
la residencia de ancianos *old people's home*
sabio *knowledgeable*
el seguro de vida *life insurance*
senil *senile*
la senilidad *senility*
la soledad *loneliness*
la tercera edad *(euph)* *senior citizens*

el cuidado de los ancianos *care of the elderly*
ahorrar para la jubilación *to save for retirement*
adaptarse a la jubilación *to adjust to retirement*
estar encerrado en casa *to be house-bound*
estar en una silla de ruedas *to be in a wheelchair*
contribuir a la sociedad *to contribute to society*
una persona de edad *(euph)* *an elderly person*
actividades para la tercera edad *activities for the elderly*
jubilarse anticipadamente *to take early retirement*
el envejecimiento de la población *the ageing of the population*
el servicio de comidas a domicilio *meals on wheels*

La Familia

el abuso de menores *child abuse*
el acogimiento familiar *fostering*
la ayuda familiar por hijos *child benefit*
la au-pair *au-pair*
el bebé *baby*
el/la canguro *baby-sitter*
el centro psicopedagógico *child guidance centre*
el clan familiar/la familia ampliada *extended family*
criar una familia *to raise a family*
dar el pecho *to breast-feed*
la descendencia *offspring*
divorciarse *to divorce*

la educación de los hijos	*upbringing of children*
la familia adoptiva	*foster home*
la familia monoparental	*single parent family*
la familia nuclear	*nuclear family*
los gemelos	*twins*
el hijo adoptivo	*adopted child*
la madre soltera	*single mother*
la madrastra	*stepmother*
la madrina	*godmother*
la maternidad	*motherhood*
el maltrato de los hijos	*child cruelty*
el mayor	*the eldest*
el menor	*the youngest*
la niñera	*nanny*
el padrastro	*stepfather*
el padre soltero	*single father*
el padrino	*godfather*
la paternidad	*fatherhood, parenthood*
el pedófilo	*paedophile*
la sobreprotección	*overprotection*
los valores familiares	*family values*
el tutor	*guardian*

crear una familia	*to start a family*
crecer en un ambiente estable	*to be brought up in a stable environment*
tener una infancia feliz	*to have a happy childhood*
el conflicto entre padres e hijos	*parent-child conflict*
tener en cuenta las circunstancias familiares	*to take the family background into account*
una política de apoyo a las familias	*family-friendly policy*
sufrir abuso	*to suffer abuse*
mostrar autoridad	*to show authority*
criar a tus hijos	*to bring up your children*

CÓMO AMPLIAR TU VOCABULARIO

El buen uso de los adjetivos es siempre muy útil para dar más vida a tus composiciones. Para aprender nuevos adjetivos prueba el siguiente juego:

Juega con tu compañero: Piensa en un adjetivo, p.ej. *suave*; después piensa en algo que el adjetivo pueda describir, p.ej. *chaqueta* y díselo a tu compañero. Él/ella deberá tratar de adivinar el adjetivo. Si no lo adivina en tres intentos, debes darle el nombre de otro objeto que pueda ser descrito con el mismo adjetivo, p.ej. *pelo*.

Ej: A: Chaqueta.
B: ¿Una chaqueta *grande*?
A: No.
B: ¿Una chaqueta *gruesa*?
A: No.
B: ¿Una chaqueta *elegante*?
A: No. Pelo.
B: ¿Un pelo *suave*?
A: ¡Correcto!

¡Cuando tu compañero lo adivine, es tu turno!

DIRECCIONES ÚTILES EN INTERNET

http://www.mujeractual.com (información para la mujer)

http://www.mtas.es/mujer/becas.htm (becas del Instituto de la Mujer)

http://www.megasitio.com/mujer (portal muy completo y fácil de utilizar sobre la mujer)

http://www.excite.es/directory/directory/010504 (directorio de sitios sobre derechos de la mujer)

http://www.cje.org (web general sobre juventud: entidades, actividades, campañas educativas y preventivas)

http://www.terra.es/personal/sussosuso/juventud.html (lista de direcciones sobre diversos Consejos de la Juventud y asociaciones de interés)

http://www.unicef.org/voy/es (propone temas de debate sobre la juventud)

http://www.asociaciones.mundivia.es/unate (programa universitario para la tercera edad)

http://www.saludpublica.com/titulos/adolescencia.htm (Adolescencia y salud. Programas sanitarios relacionados con la adolescencia)

LA DIVERSIDAD: –INMIGRACIÓN Y RACISMO–

La Inmigración

adaptarse *to fit in*
la aduana *customs*
aislarse *to isolate yourself*
el asilo político *political asylum*
bilingüe *bilingual*
buscar asilo *to seek asylum*
el campamento de refugiados *refugee camp*
la ciudadanía *citizenship*
el ciudadano *citizen*
la concesión de la nacionalidad *granting of nationality*
el conciudadano *fellow citizen*
convivir *to live together*
la deportación *deportation*
el derecho al voto *the right to vote*
desconcertado *bewildered*
las dificultades con la lengua *language difficulties*
la emigración *emigration*
el emigrante *emigrant*
emigrar *to emigrate*
establecerse *to settle down*
étnico *ethnic*
exiliado *exiled*
exiliar *to exile*
el exilio *exile*
la explotación *exploitation*
la frontera *border*
el gueto *ghetto*
la inadaptación *failure to adjust*
la inmigración *immigration*
el inmigrante *immigrant*
el inmigrante clandestino/ilegal *illegal immigrant*
inmigrar *to immigrate*
instalarse *to settle*
la integración *integration*
integrarse en la comunidad *to integrate into the community*
la ley de extranjería *(approx.) immigration laws*
las mafias de tráfico humano *human trafficking gangs*
el matrimonio de conveniencia *marriage of convenience*
el matrimonio mixto *mixed marriage*
la minoría étnica *ethnic minority*
el modo de vida *way of life*
la nacionalidad *nationality*
la naturalización *naturalization*
el país adoptivo *country of adoption*

el país anfitrión *host country*
el país de origen *country of origin*
la patera *small boat*
el permiso de residencia *residence permit*
el permiso de trabajo *work permit*
el proceso integrador *process of integration*
el refugiado *refugee*
el refugiado político *political refugee*
el refugio para inmigrantes *inmigrants' hostel*
la segunda generación *second generation*
la sociedad pluricultural *multicultural society*
la solicitud de asilo *application for asylum*
las tradiciones *traditions*
el visado *visa*
el visitante *visitor*

pedir asilo político	*to ask for political asylum*
entrar ilegalmente	*to enter illegally*
integrarse en la sociedad	*to integrate into society*
ser mano de obra barata	*to be a cheap workforce*
concesión de la nacionalidad española	*granting of Spanish nationality*
mejorar el nivel de vida	*to improve one's standard of living*
superar las barreras lingüísticas	*to overcome the linguistic barriers*
no ser capaz de adaptarse a	*to be unable to adapt oneself to*
hacer un esfuerzo para adaptarse a	*to try to adapt oneself to*
cruzar la frontera ilegalmente	*to cross the border illegally*
obtener la nacionalidad española	*to become a Spanish national*
aprender español como una lengua extranjera	*to learn Spanish as a foreign language*
cruzar el Estrecho de Gibraltar en patera	*to cross the Straits of Gibraltar in a small boat*
ponen en peligro su propia vida	*they put their own life in danger*
estar indocumentado	*not to have any identity papers*

El Racismo

el acento *accent*
la agresión *aggression*
antisemita *anti-Semitic*
el antisemitismo *anti-Semitism*
apalear *to beat up*
el cabeza rapada *skinhead*
el color de la piel *skin colour*
los derechos humanos *human rights*
la desconfianza *distrust*
la desigualdad *inequality*
el dialecto *dialect*
la discriminación racial *racial discrimination*
discriminar *to discriminate*
el disturbio racista *racist riot*
la diversidad cultural *cultural diversity*
el grupo étnico *ethnic group*
la humillación *humilliation*
humillar *to humiliate*
la identidad cultural *cultural identity*
el incendio provocado *arson attack*
incitar *to incite*
insultar *to taunt*
intimidar *to intimidate*
la intolerancia *intolerance*
la manifestación *demonstration*
la marginación *rejection*
marginado *rejected*
marginar *to reject*
el motivo *motive*
el nativo *native*
neonazi *neonazi*
el odio a los extranjeros *hatred of foreigners*
oprimir *to oppress*
el patriotismo *patriotism*
la persecución *persecution*
el prejuicio *prejudice*
la presión social *social pressure*
el racismo *racism*
racista *racist*
rechazar *to reject*
repatriar *to repatriate*
el sarcasmo *sarcasm*
la segregación racial *racial segregation*
la supresión *suppression*
el terror *terror*
la ultraderecha *extreme right-wing*
el/la ultraderechista *extreme right-winger*
la violencia racista *racial violence*
la xenofobia *xenophobia*
xenófobo *xenophobic*

tener prejuicios raciales	*to be racially prejudiced*
ser un ciudadano de segunda categoría	*to be a second-class citizen*
el brote de racismo	*outburst of racism*
la necesidad de una campaña antirracista	*the need for an anti-racist campaign*
convivir en armonía	*to live together harmoniously*
los sentimientos racistas	*racist feelings*
sentirse marginado	*to feel rejected*
la capacidad de vivir juntos	*ability to live together*
vivir en una sociedad multirracial	*to live in a multiracial society*
el respeto a la dignidad humana	*respect for human dignity*
un número creciente de ataques racistas	*a growing number of racist attacks*
ideas de extrema derecha	*right-wing extremist ideas*
la igualdad de oportunidades para las minorías étnicas en el trabajo	*equal opportunities for ethnic minorities in the workplace*

Cómo ampliar tu vocabulario

Cuando busques el significado de una palabra en un diccionario, fíjate en otras palabras que se pueden formar a partir de ella.

P.ej: *democracia*

democracia demócrata democráticamente democrático democratización democratizador democratizar

Así que, cuando mires una palabra en el diccionario, es una buena idea comprobar las palabras que van antes y después de la que estés buscando.

Busca en tu diccionario las palabras: *tolerar, exiliado, oprimir.* Comprueba su significado y el de las palabras que veas antes o después de éstas y que tengan que ver con ellas. Cuando lo hayas hecho, intenta escribir una definición de cada una de ellas en **español.** ¡Es una forma muy rápida de aumentar tu vocabulario y de facilitar el aprendizaje!

Direcciones útiles en Internet

http://www.epitelio.org/spanishv/base-es.htm.es (sobre minorías étnicas)

http://www.seg-social.es/imserso/ (Instituto de Migraciones y Servicios Sociales)

http://www.inmigra.com (asociación para la integración y amparo del inmigrante)

LA EDUCACIÓN

LA ESCOLARIDAD

la actividad cultural *cultural activity*

la actividad extraescolar *out-of-school activity*

el año académico *the academic year*

la asignatura *subject*

la asistencia a la escuela *school attendance*

la asociación de padres *parents' association*

el autobús escolar *school bus*

el Bachillerato *qualification equivalent to GCSE*

el boletín escolar *school report*

la capacidad de trabajo *capacity for work*

el centro docente *educational establishment*

las clases particulares *private classes*

el claustro de profesores *(body of) teachers*

el colegial *pupil*

el compañero de clase *classmate, school friend*

el curso escolar *school year*

el director *headmaster*

la disciplina *discipline*

la Educación Primaria *primary education*

el educador *educator*

empollar (*inf*) *to swot*

el empollón (*inf*) *swot*

la escolaridad *schooling*

escolarizar *to provide schooling*

la E.S.O. (Enseñanza Secundaria Obligatoria) *compulsory secondary schooling*

la excursión escolar *school trip*

extracurricular *outside the curriculum*

la FP (Formación Profesional) *technical education*

el horario *timetable*

el informe *report*

la jornada de puertas abiertas *parents' evening*

las materias obligatorias *compulsory subjects*

matricularse *to enrol (for a course etc.)*

mixto *mixed*

la motivación *motivation*

el niño en edad escolar *school-age child*

la orientación *guidance*

el parvulario *play school*
pasar de curso *to move up a year*
el pedagogo *pedagogue*
el plan de estudios *syllabus*
el profesor *teacher*
el profesor suplente *supply teacher*
la proporción alumno-profesor *staff-student ratio*
el rendimiento escolar *school performance*
repetir curso *to repeat a year*
el sistema educativo *educational system*
el trimestre *term*
el uniforme escolar *school uniform*
las vacaciones escolares *school holidays*

los nuevos métodos de enseñanza	*the new teaching methods*
adecuado a las aptitudes del alumno	*suited to the aptitudes of the student*
lograr un mejor rendimiento escolar	*to improve the students' performance*
mejorar la calidad de enseñanza	*to improve the quality of education*
tener en cuenta las capacidades individuales	*to take into account individual abilities*
la escolaridad es gratuita	*schooling is free*
elevar el fin de la escolaridad obligatoria	*to raise the school-leaving age*
ir bien en los estudios	*to do well in one´s studies*
el porcentaje de escolaridad es elevado	*the school population is high*
la escolaridad obligatoria hasta los 16 años	*compulsory schooling up to 16*
en las aulas	*in the classrooms*
motivar a los alumnos	*to motivate the students*

TIPOS DE CENTROS DE ENSEÑANZA

la academia *academy*
el centro concertado *state-aided private school or college*
el centro de educación especial *special needs school*
la escuela de artes y oficios *technical school*
la escuela de educación infantil *kindergarten*

la escuela de enseñanza primaria *primary school*
la escuela de formación profesional *polytechnic*
la escuela de pago *fee-paying school*
la escuela nocturna *night school*
la escuela privada *private school*
la escuela pública *state school*
la escuela unitaria *school having one teacher*
el instituto de enseñanza secundaria *comprehensive school*
el internado *boarding school*
la universidad *university*

LOS EXÁMENES

aprobar *to pass*
copiar *to copy, to cheat*
la chuleta *(inf)* *crib*
la evaluación *assessment*
la evaluación continua *continuous assessment*
el examen oral/escrito *oral/ written examination*
el éxito académico *academic success*
las notas *marks*
la prueba *test*
la recuperación *retake*
revisar *to revise*
sacar/tener un sobresaliente *to get/have an 'excellent'*
sacar/tener un notable *to get/have a 'very good'*
sacar/tener un bien *to get/have a 'good'*
sacar/tener un suficiente *to get/have a 'satisfactory'*
sacar/tener un insuficiente *to get/have an 'unsatisfactory'*
sacar/tener un muy deficiente *get/have a 'very poor'*
sacar una buena/mala nota *to get a good/bad mark*
soplar (*inf*) *to whisper (answers in an exam)*
suspender *to fail*
el test *test*

tenía la mente en blanco *my mind went blank*
el examen de ingreso *entrance examination*
presentarse a un examen *to sit an examination*
el boletín de calificaciones *school report*

Problemas En La Educación

el absentismo escolar *truancy*
abusar (de alguien) *to bully (someone)*
el abusón (*inf*) *bully*
el alborotador *troublemaker*
el ataque *attack*
autoritario *authoritarian*
la bronca *telling-off*
castigar *to punish*
el castigo (corporal) *(corporal) punishment*
copiar *to cheat*
defenderse *to defend oneself*
la expulsión *expulsion*
la falta de escolaridad *lack of schooling*
faltar a clase *to skip lessons*
faltar al respeto *to be disrespectful*
el fracaso escolar *failure at school*
hacer novillos *to play truant*
el mal comportamiento *bad behaviour*
la masificación *overcrowding*
la paliza *beating*
la pelea *fight*
perjudicial *damaging*
los problemas escolares *problems at school*
sobrecargado *overloaded*

En La Universidad

el año sabático *sabbatical year*
el área (de estudio) *field (of study)*
la beca *grant*
el becario *scholarship holder*
el catedrático *professor*
el colegio mayor *hall of residence*
el diploma *diploma*
diplomarse *to get a degree (3 years)*
el doctorado *doctorate*
la enseñanza universitaria *university education*
la facultad *faculty*
la financiación de los estudios *financing of studies*
la formación pedagógica *teacher training*
el grupo de estudio *study group*
la investigación *research*
el lector *foreign language assistant*
licenciarse *to get a degree (4 years)*
la licenciatura *degree*
la selección *selection*
la selectividad *university entrance exams*
el semestre *semester*
el servicio de alojamiento *accommodation service*

no tener perspectivas	*to have no prospects*
perder la independencia	*to lose independence*
echar del trabajo a alguien	*to give somebody the sack/to sack somebody*
la despidieron por reducción de plantilla	*she was made redundant*
suprimir puestos de trabajo	*to axe jobs*
la economía sumergida (paralela)	*the black economy*
estar buscando empleo	*to be on the lookout for a job/to be looking for a job*

La Búsqueda De Trabajo

el anuncio de trabajo	*job advert*
el aspirante	*applicant*
la carta adjunta	*covering letter*
las condiciones de empleo	*conditions of employment*
el contrato de trabajo	*work contract*
el currículum/currículo	*curriculum vitae*
el departamento de personal	*personnel department*
la descripción del trabajo	*job description*
la entrevista	*interview*
entrevistar	*to interview*
la experiencia laboral	*work experience*
la hoja de solicitud	*application form*
el mercado de trabajo	*job market*
la oferta de empleo	*job offer*
la oposición	*competitive examination*
las perspectivas de trabajo	*job prospects*
el rechazo	*rejection*
la recomendación	*testimonial*
la referencia	*reference*
el solicitante	*applicant*
la solicitud	*application*
la titulación	*qualifications*

opositar a algo	*to sit a competitive examination*
solicitar un puesto de trabajo en X	*to apply for a job at X*
X dará referencias sobre mí	*X is acting as my referee*
enviar carta explicatoria y currículo a X	*to send a covering letter and curriculum vitae to X*
hemos escogido a X para el puesto	*we have chosen X for the job*

emplear a alguien	*to take someone on*
una compañía me ha ofrecido un puesto	*I have been offered a job by a company*
buena suerte en tu nuevo trabajo	*good luck in your new job*
entró en la empresa por enchufe (*inf*)	*he got into the company through connections*

En La Oficina

el archivo	*file*
la centralita	*switchboard*
el clasificador	*filing cabinet*
la competencia	*competition*
la conexión telefónica	*telephone connection*
el contestador automático	*answerphone*
el despacho	*office*
la documentación	*documentation*
la extensión	*extension*
el facsímil (fax)	*facsimile (fax)*
la fotocopiadora	*photocopier*
el inalámbrico	*cordless*
el interfono	*interphone*
la llamada internacional	*international call*
la llamada telefónica	*phone call*
mandar por fax	*to fax*
la ofimática	*office automation*
poner con	*to put through to (on phone)*
por teléfono	*by phone*
el prefijo	*dialling code*
el procesador de textos	*word processor*
el regalo promocional	*promotional gift*
la taquigrafía	*shorthand*
la tarjeta comercial	*business card*
el teléfono móvil	*mobile phone*
el vehículo de la empresa	*company car*
la vídeoconferencia	*video conference*

El Mundo Del Trabajo

el año sabático	*sabbatical year*
el área de responsabilidad	*area of responsibility*
el ascenso	*promotion*
el aumento de sueldo	*pay rise*
la baja maternal	*maternity leave*
la baja retribuida	*paid leave*
la burocracia	*bureaucracy*
el comité de empresa	*works committee*
la competitividad	*competitiveness*

las condiciones de trabajo — *working conditions*
la conferencia — *conference*
confidencial — *confidential*
el conflicto salarial — *wage dispute*
contratar — *to employ*
la cooperación — *co-operation*
la degradación — *demotion*
el departamento — *department*
el día de paga — *pay day*
la discriminación sexual — *sex discrimination*
emplear — *to employ*
estar en huelga — *to be on strike*
los gastos de transporte — *travel expenses*
la guardería — *crèche*
las horas extras — *overtime*
el horario flexible — *flexi-time*
la incapacidad laboral — *unfitness for work*
la jerarquía — *hierarchy*
la junta general — *general meeting*
negociar — *to negotiate*
las negociaciones — *negotiations*
las normas de seguridad — *safety regulations*
la oficina central — *head office*
el período de prueba — *probationary period*
la profesión — *profession*
el profesional — *professional*
reivindicar — *to claim*
la responsabilidad — *responsibility*
la reunión general — *general meeting*
el salario — *salary*
el seminario — *seminar*
los servicios de administración — *management services*
el sindicato — *union*
la tarea — *job, task*
trabajar en el extranjero — *to work abroad*
el trabajo de jornada completa — *full-time job*
el trabajo de media jornada — *part-time job*
el trabajo en equipo — *team work*
las vacaciones retribuidas — *paid holidays*
el viaje de negocios — *business trip*

firmar un contrato — *to sign a contract*
dar una cita — *to make an appointment*
hacer negocios con alguien — *to do business with someone*
X está de baja por enfermedad — *X is off sick*
dejar el trabajo — *to quit one's job*
trabajar por cuenta propia/ser trabajador autónomo — *to be self-employed*

convocar/desconvocar una huelga	*to call/to call off a strike*
tener un horario flexible	*to work flexitime*
estar en huelga	*to be on strike*
la congelación salarial	*wage freeze*
los derechos de los trabajadores	*workers´ rights*
el acoso sexual en el trabajo	*sexual harassment at work*

EL PERSONAL

el abastecedor	*supplier*
el accionista	*shareholder*
el agente	*agent, dealer*
el aprendiz	*apprentice*
el asalariado	*paid worker*
el asesor	*consultant*
el cliente	*customer*
el colega	*colleague*
el comprador	*purchaser*
el contable	*accountant*
la direccción	*management*
el director de personal	*personnel manager*
el director de ventas	*sales manager*
el director general	*managing director*
el empleado	*employee*
el empleado eventual	*temporary worker*
el empresario	*businessman, employer*
el encargado	*foreman*
el fabricante	*manufacturer*
la gente de negocios	*business people*
el intermediario	*middleman*
el jefe	*boss*
el líder	*leader*
el líder del equipo	*team leader*
la mano de obra	*work-force*
el obrero	*worker*
el oficinista	*office worker*
el ordenanza	*office boy*
el peón	*unskilled worker*
el personal	*staff*
la plantilla	*staff*
el propietario	*owner*
el proveedor	*supplier*
el representante	*representative*
el secretario	*secretary*
el sindicalista	*trade unionist*
el socio	*business partner*
el trabajador	*worker*
el trabajador autónomo	*self-employed person*
el vendedor	*sales assistant*

el sueldo mensual es de 200.000 pesetas netas	*the monthly salary is 200,000 pesetas net*
avisar con una semana de antelación	*to give one week's notice*
conseguir un trabajo eventual	*to get a temporary job*
recibir la paga extraordinaria de Navidad	*to get a Christmas bonus*
ser un trabajador de cuello blanco	*to be a white-collar worker*
la reducción de la jornada de trabajo	*reduction of the working day*
el derecho a la huelga	*the right to strike*

Cómo ampliar tu vocabulario

Aquí tienes un modelo de carta en español que puede usarse para pedir información sobre un tema que te interese:

Estimado/a señor/a:

Soy un/a estudiante de español en NAME OF SCHOOL/COLLEGE/UNIVERSITY. Estoy haciendo un estudio sobre NAME OF TOPIC y me dirijo a usted para solicitarle información sobre el tema.

Si usted dispone de folletos u otra documentación que pueda serme de utilidad, le estaría muy agradecido/a si pudiera enviarla a la siguiente dirección: ADDRESS OF YOUR SCHOOL/COLLEGE/UNIVERSITY.

Agradeciéndole de antemano su atención, me despido atentamente,

Lee Tate

Direcciones útiles en Internet

http://www.mtas.es/ (web del Ministerio de Trabajo y Asuntos Sociales)

http://www.infoempleo.es (ofertas de empleo y posibilidad de incluir el currículo)

http://www.trabajos.com (intercambio entre ofertas y demandas de trabajo)

http://www.webglass.com/cgsa (web dedicada a productos del mercado laboral para extranjeros)

http://www.laley.net/bdatos/menulab.htm (recopilación de textos sobre derecho laboral)

http://www.bcnred.com/trabajo (web general dedicada al empleo)

http://www.inem.es (web oficial del Instituto Nacional de Empleo)

http://www.webempleo.org (web general sobre empleo; ofertas, trabajo en el extranjero, cursos)

http://www.ugt.es (web de la Unión General de Trabajadores)

http://www.ccoo.es (web de Comisiones Obreras)

EL TIEMPO LIBRE

EL DEPORTE

el aficionado	*supporter*
agotador	*exhausting*
el ala delta	*hang-glider*
la amonestación	*warning*
apostar	*to bet*
el árbitro	*referee*
el ataque	*attack*
el atleta	*athlete*
el atletismo	*athletics*
el boxeo	*boxing*
bucear	*to skin-dive*
el calentamiento	*warm-up*
el campeón	*champion*
el campeonato	*championship*
el campo de entrenamiento	*training camp*
la cancha/pista de tenis	*tennis court*
el capitán	*captain*
la carrera	*race*
la carrera de relevos	*relay race*
el club	*club*
la competición	*competition*
competir con	*to compete against*
la copa	*cup*
el corredor de fondo	*long-distance runner*
correr	*to run*
el cuadrilátero	*(boxing) ring*
la cultura del ocio	*leisure culture*
defender	*to defend*
el defensa	*defender*
el delantero	*forward*
el deporte de equipo	*team sport*
los deportes acuáticos	*water sports*
los deportes de competición	*competitive sports*
los deportes de invierno	*winter sports*
el deportista profesional	*professional sportsperson*
derrotar	*to defeat*
descalificar	*to disqualify*
el doping	*doping, drug-taking*
el ejercicio	*exercise, movement*
eliminar	*to eliminate*
la eliminatoria	*heat*
empatar	*to draw*
el entrenador	*coach*
entrenar	*to train*
el equipo	*team*
el equipo rival	*the opposing team*
el espectador	*spectator*
el espíritu de equipo	*team spirit*
esquiar	*to ski*

el estadio	*stadium*
el éxito	*success, achievement*
expulsar	*to send off*
la falta	*foul*
el fichaje	*signing (up)*
la final	*final*
el finalista	*finalist*
la gimnasia	*gymnastics*
el hincha	*supporter*
el hipódromo	*racetrack*
invencible	*unbeatable*
el juego sucio	*foul play*
el juez de silla	*umpire (tennis)*
el jugador nacional	*native-born player*
la medalla	*medal*
noquear	*to knock out*
el oponente	*opponent*
el participante	*participant*
el partido en casa/fuera de casa	*home/away match*
el patinaje sobre hielo	*ice skating*
el patrocinador	*sponsor*
el penalti	*penalty (kick)*
perder	*to lose*
las pistas de esquí	*ski slopes*
el polideportivo	*sports centre*
la popularidad	*popularity*
el portero	*goalkeeper*
la reaparición	*come-back*
el récord mundial	*world record*
la regla	*rule*
la resistencia	*stamina*
el resultado final	*final score*
el seguidor	*fan*
la semifinal	*semi-final*
la táctica	*tactic*
la temporada	*season*
tomar parte	*to take part*
el torneo	*tournament*
el traspaso	*transfer*
las vallas	*hurdles*
vencer	*to beat*
la victoria	*victory*
la vuelta	*lap, round*

entrenar hasta cinco horas diarias	*to train up to five hours a day*
el árbitro expulsó a X	*the referee sent X off*
la lucha por el título	*the fight for the title*
X llegó a la semifinal	*X got through to the semi-final*
el resultado era 2 a 3 al medio tiempo	*the score was 2-3 at half time*
X derrotó a Y por seis a uno	*X beat Y 6-1*
¿quién gana?	*what's the score?*

batir un récord	*to break a record*
una carrera contra reloj	*a race against the clock*
participar en una carrera	*to run a race*
hacer deporte	*to take part in sport*
los Juegos Olímpicos	*The Olympic Games*
estar fuera de juego	*to be offside*
ganar el título	*to win the title*
el resultado es empate a dos	*the result is a two-all draw*
conseguir una medalla de bronce	*to get a bronze medal*
detentar el récord mundial	*to hold the world record*
mezclar el deporte y la política	*to mix sport and politics*
marcar cinco goles	*to score five goals*
la Real Sociedad empató con el Real Madrid	*Real Sociedad drew with Real Madrid*

Las Aficiones

el aburrimiento	*boredom*
agradable	*enjoyable*
artístico	*artistic*
autodidacto	*self-taught*
el bricolage	*DIY*
la clase nocturna	*evening class*
la colección	*collection*
coleccionar	*to collect*
costoso	*costly*
distraerse *(inf)*	*to switch off*
dotado	*gifted*
la educación de adultos	*adult education*
entendido	*knowledgeable*
entusiasta	*enthusiastic*
escuchar música	*to listen to music*
la experiencia	*experience*
fanático	*fanatic*
fascinante	*fascinating*
la fotografía	*photography*
gratificante	*rewarding*
individual	*individual*
el interés	*interest*
la jardinería	*gardening*
jugar al ajedrez	*to play chess*
el miembro	*member*
musical	*musical*

ocioso	*idle*
original	*original*
la pasión	*passion*
el placer	*pleasure*
popular	*popular*
práctico	*practical*
la relajación	*relaxation*
relajarse	*to relax*
revelar fotografías	*to develop photographs*
sociable	*sociable*
el talento	*talent*
talentoso	*talented*
el tiempo libre	*free time*

hacer trabajo voluntario	*to do voluntary work*
hacer algo como una afición	*to do something as a hobby*
ser un entusiasta de algo	*to be enthusiastic about something*
aprovechar el tiempo	*to make good use of time*
aficionarse a algo	*to become fond of something*
hacer algo constructivo	*to do something constructive*
desarrollar tus aptitudes	*to develop your aptitudes*

El Turismo

la agencia de viajes	*travel agency*
el alojamiento	*accommodation*
alquilar un coche	*to hire a car*
el alquiler	*rent*
animado	*lively*
aventurero	*adventurous*
broncearse	*to get a suntan*
la cancelación	*cancellation*
la casa rural	*country house*
el centro turístico	*tourist centre*
el cheque de viaje	*traveller's cheque*
el conductor	*driver*
las costumbres	*customs*
el crucero	*cruise*
descubrir	*to discover*
el destino	*destination*
la distancia	*distance*
divertirse	*to have fun*
la estancia	*stay*
la excursión	*outing, trip*
el excursionista	*day-tripper*
explorar	*to explore*
facturar el equipaje	*to check in luggage*
el ferry	*ferry*
la fiesta	*festivity*

el fin de temporada	*end of season*
firmar el registro	*to check in (at hotel)*
el folleto de viajes	*travel brochure*
el/la guía	*guide (person)*
la guía	*guide book*
hacer autostop	*to hitch hike*
hacer turismo	*to go sightseeing*
la industria del turismo	*tourist industry*
la industria hotelera	*hotel industry*
el interés histórico	*historical interest*
irse de vacaciones	*to go away on holiday*
el itinerario	*itinerary*
el libro de reclamaciones	*complaints book*
la llegada	*arrival*
el mapa de carreteras	*route map*
marearse	*to get travel-sick*
la media pensión	*half-board*
la moneda	*currency*
montar (una tienda)	*to pitch (a tent)*
el monumento	*monument*
mundialmente famoso	*world famous*
la oferta especial	*special offer*
la oficina de turismo	*tourist office*
el pasajero	*passenger*
el pasaporte	*passport*
pasear	*to walk*
pintoresco	*picturesque*
planear	*to plan*
el precio	*price*
procedente de	*coming from*
la recepción	*check-in desk*
la reclamación	*complaint*
reclamar	*to reclaim (baggage)*
recuperarse	*to recover, to recuperate*
relajarse	*to relax*
reservar	*to reserve*
el retraso	*delay*
la sala de espera	*waiting room*
la salida	*departure*
el seguro de viaje	*travel insurance*
el suplemento	*supplement*
la temporada alta/baja	*high/low season*
tomar el sol	*to sunbathe*
el transbordador	*ferry*
el transbordo	*transfer*
el turismo de calidad	*quality tourism*
el turismo de masas	*mass tourism*
la vacunación	*vaccination*
ver mundo	*to see the world*
la vía	*platform*
el viaje en barco	*boat trip*
el viaje organizado	*package holiday*
la vida nocturna	*night life*
visitar	*to visit*
la vista	*view*
el vuelo chárter	*charter flight*
el vuelo regular	*scheduled flight*
la zona costera	*coastal area*

estar afectado por el desfase de horario	*to be affected by jetlag*
muchos puestos de trabajo dependen de la demanda turística	*many jobs rely on the demand from tourists*
el turismo constituye su mayor industria	*the tourist trade is their biggest industry*
ahora se hace más turismo que nunca	*there's more tourism than ever now*
hacer un recorrido turístico de la ciudad	*to see the sights of the city*
el turismo tiene un valor educativo	*tourism has an educational value*
alejado de la rutina diaria	*away from the daily routine*
está a tres horas de vuelo de Madrid	*it is a three-hour flight from Madrid*
el turismo de masas es un fenómeno relativamente moderno	*mass tourism is a relatively modern phenomenon*
el turismo desempeña un papel fundamental en la economía española	*tourism plays a substantial role in the Spanish economy*

CÓMO AMPLIAR TU VOCABULARIO

Cuando estés aprendiendo nuevas palabras, no siempre necesitas traducirlas al inglés. Muchas veces es mucho mejor definirlas o buscar palabras con un significado similar.

P.ej. *Polideportivo – un centro donde se pueden practicar muchos deportes.*

Prueba a hacer tus propias definiciones:

competición	*cheque de viaje*	*bucear*	*monumento*
entrenador	*pasaporte*	*jardinería*	*turismo*

De ahora en adelante, cuando aprendas nuevas palabras, piensa en una definición y anótala en tu cuaderno de vocabulario.

DIRECCIONES ÚTILES EN INTERNET

http://www.tourspain.es (organismo oficial de turismo para España)

http://www.elpais-aguilar.es/ (guías de viaje)

http://www.iberica.com/ (la más amplia base de datos turísticos sobre España)

http://www.parador.es/ (web de Paradores de España)

http://www.acampa.com/ (informacón sobre turismo rural y parques naturales)

http://www.es.sports.yahoo.com (portal dedicado al deporte)

LA CULTURA

LA LITERATURA

acentuar	*to stress*
el antihéroe	*antihero*
la antiheroína	*antiheroine*
la autobiografía	*autobiography*
el autor	*author*
el best-seller	*best-seller*
el capítulo	*chapter*
la cita	*quotation*
citar	*to quote*
la comparación	*comparison*
comparar	*to compare*
contemporáneo	*contemporary*
el crítico	*critic*
el cuento de hadas	*fairy tale*
los derechos de autor	*copyright*
el desarrollo	*development*
detallado	*detailed*
el diálogo	*dialogue*
el drama	*drama*
la edición	*edition*
la edición especial	*special edition*
editar	*to publish*
el editorial	*editorial*
la editorial	*publisher (company)*
enfatizar con	*to empathize with*
la épica	*epic*
el escritor	*author, writer*
el extracto	*excerpt*
la fábula	*fable*
la ficción	*fiction*
la figura	*character*
el filósofo	*philosopher*
el final feliz	*happy ending*
el género	*genre*
el héroe	*hero*
la heroína	*heroine*
la introducción	*introduction*
la ironía	*irony*
la leyenda	*legend*
el libro de bolsillo	*pocket book*
el libro de tapa dura	*hardback*
el libro en rústica	*paperback*
la lírica	*poetry*
la literatura no novelesca	*non-fiction*
la metáfora	*metaphor*
la moral	*moral*
el narrador	*narrator*
la narrativa	*narrative*
la novela	*novel*
la novela policíaca	*detective story*
la novela romántica	*romantic novel*
la obra maestra	*masterpiece*
la opinión	*opinion, view*
el párrafo	*paragraph*
el pensamiento	*thought*
el personaje	*character*

el poema	*poem*
la poesía	*poetry*
el poeta/la poetisa	*poet*
poético	*poetic*
el prefacio	*preface*
la prosa	*prose*
publicar	*to publish*
el realismo	*realism*
la reimpresión	*reprint*
retratar	*to portray*
la rima	*rhyme*
rimar	*to rhyme*
el romanticismo	*romanticism*
satírico	*satirical*
simbólico	*symbolic*
el símil	*simile*
el surrealismo	*surrealism*
el tema central	*leitmotif*
la tirada	*print-run*
el tópico	*cliché*
la traducción	*translation*
la versión íntegra	*unabridged version*
el verso	*verse*
el volumen	*volume*

la última obra	*the latest work*
escrito en un estilo vivo	*written in a lively style*
las obras de los treinta a los sesenta	*works from the thirties to the sixties*
un autor conocido en toda Europa	*an author known throughout Europe*
narrado con ironía	*narrated with irony*
el libro publicado en 1998	*the book published in 1998*
en español	*in Spanish*
escrito en primera/tercera persona	*written in the first/third person*

El Teatro

abuchear	*to boo*
los accesorios	*props*
el actor	*actor*
la actriz	*actress*
la actuación	*acting*
aparecer	*to appear*
la aparición	*appearance*
el aplauso	*applause*
el argumento	*plot*
la atmósfera	*atmosphere*
el cambio de escenario	*scene change*
la comedia	*comedy, play, drama*
comunicar	*to convey*
el decorado	*scenery*
el descanso	*interval*
el desenlace	*denouement*
el destino	*fate*
la dirección	*direction*

dirigir	*to direct*
el drama	*drama*
dramático	*dramatic*
el dramaturgo	*dramatist*
el ensayo general	*dress rehearsal*
entre bastidores *(adv)*	*backstage*
el escenario	*stage*
el espectáculo	*performance*
el espectáculo de variedades	*variety show*
estrenar	*to perform for the first time*
el estreno	*first night*
expresar	*to express*
la figura	*figure*
la función	*performance*
el lleno	*full house*
el miedo escénico	*stage fright*
la obra (de teatro)	*play*
el preestreno	*preview*
el premier	*première*
el primer acto	*first act*
poner en escena	*to put on stage*
el programa	*programme*
el protagonista	*protagonist*
el público	*audience*
el reparto	*cast*
la representación	*production*
representar	*to portray*
el tema	*theme*
el tema central	*main theme*
la tragedia	*tragedy*
la tragicomedia	*tragicomedy*
el tramoyista	*stagehand*
el vestuario	*wardrobe, dressing room*

la obra trata de...	*the play is about ...*
tiene lugar en el siglo XVI	*it takes place in the 16th century*
el personaje central de esta historia	*the central character of this story*
la escena tiene lugar en X	*the scene takes place in X*
ganar el Premio Nobel de Literatura	*to win the Nobel Prize for Literature*
estar en el escenario	*to be on stage*
ella hizo el papel de Isolda	*she played the part of Isolde*
X siempre está siendo puesto en escena	*X is always being staged*
ir de gira	*to go on tour*
ganó un premio	*it won a prize*
una representación exitosa	*a successful production/performance*
interpretar una obra	*to perform a play*
mantiene el interés del público	*holds the audience's attention*
una comedia innovadora	*an innovative comedy*
el mensaje de esta obra es	*this play's message is*

El Cine

la banda sonora	*sound track*
el cine	*cinema*
el cineasta	*film-maker*
el cinéfilo	*cinemagoer*
la continuación	*sequel*
la coproducción	*co-production*
la dirección	*direction*
dirigir	*to direct*
el distribuidor	*distributor*
doblar	*to dub*
los efectos especiales	*special effects*
los efectos sonoros	*sound effects*
en cámara lenta	*in slow motion*
la estrella de cine	*film star*
estrenar	*to release*
el éxito de taquilla	*box-office hit*
los exteriores	*location*
filmar	*to shoot*
el guión	*script*
hacer un papel	*to play a role, to take a part*
no apta para menores	*for adults only*
la pantalla	*screen*
el papel	*role*
el papel principal	*leading role*
el papel secundario	*supporting role*
la película en blanco y negro	*black and white film*
la película muda	*silent film*
el plató	*set*
presentar	*to present*
el primer plano	*close-up*
el productor	*producer*
el rodaje	*filming*
rodar	*to film*
la toma	*shot*
el trailer	*trailer*

para todos los públicos	*suitable for all ages*
él estaba en esta película	*he was in this film*
la película tiene subtítulos en español	*the film has Spanish subtitles*
la película se está proyectando por todo el mundo	*the film is showing all over the world*
una película en cuatro partes	*a film in four parts*
la película no es fiel al libro	*the film does not stick to the book*
adaptada para el cine	*adapted for the cinema*
estar rodando exteriores	*to be on location*
ver una película	*to watch a film*

basada en la novela X del mismo nombre	*based on the novel X of the same name*
por el ganador del Oscar X	*by the Oscar-winning X*
pronto en estas pantallas	*coming soon to this cinema*
se mantuvo en cartelera durante dos años	*it ran for two years*

LA DANZA

actuar	*to perform*
el bailaor	*flamenco dancer*
bailar claqué	*to tap dance*
el bailarín	*dancer*
el baile de salón	*ballroom dancing*
el ballet	*ballet*
la compañía	*company*
la coordinación	*co-ordination*
la coreografía	*choreography*
el coreógrafo	*choreographer*
la danza jazz	*jazz dance*
el movimiento	*movement*
la primera bailarina	*prima ballerina*

recibir clases de ballet	*to take ballet lessons*
formación en danza contemporánea	*training in contemporary dance*
la danza moderna	*modern dance*

EL ARTE

abstracto	*abstract*
el aguafuerte	*etching*
las artes gráficas	*graphic arts*
el artista	*artist*
el aspecto	*aspect*
las bellas artes	*fine arts*
el bodegón	*still life*
el bosquejo	*sketch*
la colección	*collection*
el cuadro original	*original painting*
el dibujo	*drawing*
el diseño	*design*
el escultor	*sculptor*
la escultura	*sculpture*
el estudio	*studio*
la exposición	*exhibition*
el fondo	*background*
la fotografía	*photography*
la galería	*gallery*
el grabado	*engraving*
la imitación	*imitation*

inmortalizar	*to immortalize*
el lienzo	*canvas*
el objeto	*object*
la obra de arte	*work of art*
el paisaje	*landscape*
la perspectiva	*perspective*
el pincel	*brush*
la pintura a la acuarela	*watercolour*
la pintura al óleo	*oil painting*
representar	*to represent*
el retrato	*portrait*
la retrospectiva	*retrospective (exhibition)*
la vanguardia	*forefront*

el arte moderno	*modern art*
un talento prometedor	*a promising talent*
expresa algo muy importante	*it expresses something very important*
pintar con pintura al óleo	*to paint in oils*

La Música

el altavoz	*loudspeaker*
la armonía	*harmony*
la canción	*song*
el/la cantante	*singer*
el canto	*singing*
la composición	*composition*
el compositor	*composer*
compuesto por	*composed by*
el coro	*choir*
el cuarteto	*quartet*
el director (de orquesta)	*conductor*
el disco compacto	*CD*
ensayar	*to rehearse*
el ensayo	*rehearsal*
la estrella de pop	*pop star*
el grupo de rock	*rock band*
la guitarra eléctrica	*electric guitar*
improvisar	*to improvise*
instrumental	*instrumental*
instrumentar	*to orchestrate*
el instrumento	*instrument*
los instrumentos de cuerda	*stringed instruments*
los instrumentos de metal	*brass instruments*
el jazz	*jazz*
la lista de éxitos	*charts*
la melodía	*melody*
melódico	*melodic*
el melómano	*music lover*
el mezclador de sonido	*sound mixer*
la música folk	*folk music*
el músico	*musician*

la ópera	*opera*
la orquesta	*orchestra*
la ovación	*ovation*
la partitura	*score (musical)*
el pentagrama	*staff*
la pieza musical	*piece of music*
el recital	*recital*
el ritmo	*rhythm*
la sala de conciertos	*concert hall*
el sencillo	*single*
la sinfonía	*symphony*
solfear	*to sol-fa*
el solfeo	*sol-fa*
el solista	*soloist*
el sonido	*sound*
el virtuoso	*virtuoso*
el vocalista	*vocalist*
la zarzuela	*Spanish operetta*

X está en la lista de éxitos esta semana	*X is in the charts this week*
X es número uno	*X is number one*
sacar un nuevo álbum	*to release a new album*
practicar regularmente	*to practise regularly*
repentizar/leer música	*to sight-read/to read music*
música clásica/contemporánea	*classical/contemporary music*
en cuatro movimientos	*in four movements*
tocar de oído	*to play by ear*
X dirige la orquesta esta noche	*X is conducting the orchestra tonight*

La Crítica

agradable	*enjoyable*
ambicioso	*ambitious*
asombroso	*amazing*
atmosférico	*atmospheric*
complicado	*complicated*
conmovedor	*moving*
convincente	*convincing*
decepcionante	*disappointing*
desastroso	*disastrous*
divertido	*amusing*
efectivo	*effective*
encantador	*charming*
entretenido	*entertaining*
espléndido	*splendid*
eterno	*eternal*
excitante	*exciting*
exitoso	*successful*

experimental	*experimental*	loable	*praiseworthy*
expresivo	*expressive*	magnífico	*magnificent*
extraordinario	*remarkable*	mediocre	*mediocre*
flojo de argumento	*thin on plot*	nuevo	*new*
genial	*brilliant*	objetivo	*objective*
histórico	*historic*	opresivo	*oppressive*
impresionante	*impressive*	peculiar	*unique*
inexpresivo	*inexpressive*	preciso	*accurate*
innovador	*innovative*	prometedor	*promising*
interesante	*interesting*	sentimental	*sentimental*
inusual	*unusual*	serio	*serious*
lacrimógeno	*tear-jerking*	subjetivo	*subjective*
lleno de acción	*action-packed*	trivial	*trivial*

tener un enorme éxito	*to be a big hit*
tener buenas críticas	*to get good reviews*
X tuvo una actuación irrepetible	*X gave a once-in-a-lifetime performance*
me dejé llevar por la obra	*I was carried along by the play*
corriente y moliente (*inf*)	*run-of-the-mill*

DIRECCIONES ÚTILES EN INTERNET

http://www.museoprado.meu.es (información sobre el Museo del Prado)

http://www.guggenheim-bilbao.es (lo mejor del arte del Museo Guggenheim)

http://www.mcu.es/bpe/bpe.html (página web del Ministerio de Educación donde se pueden consultar las bibliotecas públicas)

http://www.uchile.cl/actividades_culturales/premios_nobel/neruda/pablo_neruda.html (selección de fotografías de Neruda y sus poemas)

http://www.buscacine.com/ (base de datos de páginas de cine en español)

http://www.musica.org/ (servicio informativo de la realidad musical española)

http://www.infoescena.es (web dedicada al teatro, la danza y la música. Muy buena)

http://www.ciudadfutura.com/rickymartin (página dedicada a Ricky Martin)

CÓMO AMPLIAR TU VOCABULARIO

Cuando estés aprendiendo un grupo de palabras pertenecientes a un mismo campo semántico, divídelas en diferentes secciones.

P.ej., dentro del tema *arte,* puedes hacer la siguiente clasificación:

persona que realiza la acción: artista	*resultado de la acción: obra*	*con que se realiza: material*	*acción: actividad*
pintor	*pintura*	*lienzo* *pincel* *paleta* *pintura* *caballete*	*pintar*
diseñador	*diseño*	*lápiz* *ordenador* *papel*	*diseñar*
músico	*canción* *ópera* *sinfonía*	*violín* *piano* *órgano*	*tocar* *interpretar*

También puedes clasificar los adjetivos en negativos y positivos.

P.ej., en el tema *La cultura*:

positivos	*negativos*
agradable	*desagradable*
divertido	*aburrido*
impresionante	*decepcionante*

Cada vez que aprendas una palabra acuérdate de apuntarla en tu cuaderno de vocabulario y de hacer una frase donde uses la nueva palabra.

LA SALUD

EL TABACO

el alquitrán *tar*
antisocial *antisocial*
el anuncio de tabaco *cigarette advert*
bajo en nicotina *low-nicotine*
la calada *puff*
el cáncer de pulmón/de garganta *lung/throat cancer*
el cigarrillo *cigarette*
la colilla *stub*
las dificultades respiratorias *breathing difficulties*
el fumador *smoker*
el fumador pasivo *passive smoker*
fumar *to smoke*
el hábito *habit*
inhalar *to inhale*
la nicotina *nicotine*
el parche de nicotina *nicotine patch*
la pipa *pipe*
el pitillo *(inf)* *fag*
el puro *cigar*
el tabaquismo *addiction to tobacco*
la tos del fumador *smoker's cough*

el tabaco perjudica seriamente la salud *tobacco seriously damages health*
fumar diez cigarrillos al día *to smoke ten cigarettes a day*
la campaña antitabaco *anti-smoking campaign*
ser un fumador empedernido *to be a heavy smoker*
la habitación está llena de humo *the room is full of smoke*
dejar de fumar *to give up smoking*

LA DROGA

el abuso de las drogas *drug abuse*
la adicción *addiction*
la adicción a la heroína *heroin addiction*
el adicto a la droga *drug addict*
la alucinación *hallucination*
la brigada de estupefacientes *drug squad*
el camello *(sl)* *drug pusher*
la campaña anti-drogas *anti-drugs campaign*
el centro de rehabilitación *rehabilitation centre*
la cocaína *cocaine*

el cocainómano	*cocaine addict*
colocado *(sl)*	*high (on drugs)*
el consumo de drogas	*drug taking*
desintoxicar	*to treat for drug addiction*
la dosis	*dose*
las drogas de diseño	*designer drugs*
el drogadicto	*drug taker*
drogarse	*to take drugs*
el efecto	*effect*
esnifar *(sl)*	*to sniff*
el éxtasis	*ecstasy*
el hachís	*hashish*
la heroína	*heroin*
el heroinómano	*heroin addict*
la hierba *(sl)*	*grass*
intravenoso	*intravenous*
inyectar	*to inject*
la jeringuilla	*syringe*
la legalización	*legalisation*
el mono *(sl)*	*withdrawal symptoms*
el narcótico	*narcotic*
el narcotraficante	*drug trafficker*
el narcotráfico	*drugs traffic*
el perro antidroga	*sniffer dog*
el pico *(sl)*	*shot*
el porro *(sl)*	*joint*
la rehabilitación	*rehabilitation*
el riesgo de infección	*risk of infection*
el síndrome de abstinencia	*withdrawal syndrome*
la sobredosis	*overdose*
el traficante de droga	*drug dealer*
el tráfico de drogas	*drug trafficking*
el yonqui *(sl)*	*junkie*

inhalar pegamento	*to glue-sniff*
adormecer las frustraciones con...	*to calm one's frustrations with ...*
cambiar tu personalidad	*to change your personality*
sustancias dañinas que se introducen en el cuerpo	*harmful substances which get into the body*
librarse de las inhibiciones	*to blow away inhibitions*
bajo el efecto del hachís	*under the influence of hashish*
un programa de reinserción	*a programme of reintegration*
darle al porro *(sl)*	*to smoke dope regularly*
ser un esclavo de la droga	*to be a slave to drugs*
fumar un porro *(sl)*	*to smoke a joint*
ser un drogata *(sl)*	*to be a druggie*
droga blanda/dura	*soft/hard drug*
un cambio de personalidad	*a personality change*
hacer una cura de desintoxicación	*to be treated for drug addiction*

El Alcohol

el abstemio	*teetotaller*
el alcohólico	*alcoholic*
el alcoholímetro	*Breathalyser ®*
el alcoholismo	*alcoholism*
alcoholizar	*to alcoholise*
la bebida alcohólica	*alcoholic drink*
el borracho *(inf)*	*drunk*
el copeo/chateo *(inf)*	*pub crawl*
ebrio	*intoxicated*
la embriaguez	*drunkenness*
estar borracho	*to be drunk*
estar trompa *(inf)*	*to be stoned*
la excitabilidad	*excitability*
la intoxicación alcohólica	*alcohol poisoning*
la resaca	*hangover*
sobrio	*sober*
vomitar	*to be sick*

inducir a alguien a la bebida	*to drive somebody to drink*
bajo los efectos del alcohol	*under the influence of alcohol*
si bebes no conduzcas	*don't drink and drive*
0,8 ml de alcohol en la sangre	*0.8 ml of alcohol in the blood*
darse a la bebida	*to go on the booze*
estar como una cuba *(inf)*	*to be stoned*
el abuso del alcohol entre los jóvenes	*excessive drinking amongst the young*

El Sida

el análisis de sangre	*blood test*
los anticuerpos del SIDA	*HIV antibodies*
el banco de sangre	*blood bank*
la célula	*cell*
el condón/preservativo	*condom*
diagnosticar	*to diagnose*
el donante de sangre	*blood donor*
el enfermo de sida	*AIDS sufferer*
la epidemia	*outbreak*
el hemofílico	*haemophiliac*
el homosexual	*homosexual*
incurable	*incurable*
infectar	*to infect*
infectado con el VIH	*HIV infected*
la inmunodeficiencia	*immune deficiency*
la mutación	*mutation*
la prevención	*prevention*
la promiscuidad	*promiscuity*
propagarse	*to spread*
la prueba del SIDA	*AIDS test*

la sangre contaminada *contaminated blood*
seronegativo *HIV negative*
seropositivo *HIV positive*
el síndrome *syndrome*
el sistema inmunológico *immune system*
la transfusión de sangre *blood transfusion*
la unidad de enfermos de SIDA *AIDS ward*

pasar el virus a la pareja	*to pass the virus on to a sexual partner*
un cambio en el comportamiento sexual	*a change in sexual behaviour*
morir de SIDA	*to die of AIDS*
contraer el virus	*to contract the virus*
la enfermedad puede transmitirse a través de	*the disease can be transmitted by*
un medio para combatir la enfermedad	*a means of combating the virus*

El Aborto

abortar *to have an abortion/miscarriage*
el abortista/anti-abortista *abortion/anti-abortion campaigner*
el embarazo no deseado *unwanted pregnancy*
el embrión *embryo*
el feto *foetus*
la gestación *gestation*
la interrupción del embarazo *termination of pregnancy*
legalizar *to legalise*
la orientación *counselling*
la prueba de embarazo *pregnancy test*
punible *punishable*
la violación *rape*

aborto clandestino	*backstreet abortion*
razones para la interrupción del embarazo	*reasons for termination*
asesoramiento cualificado de la mujer embarazada	*qualified counselling for the pregnant woman*
legalización del aborto	*legalisation of abortion*
la campaña contra el aborto	*anti-abortion campaign*

malformaciones en el feto	*malformation in the foetus*
campaña para la despenalización del aborto	*campaign for the decriminalisation of abortion*
matar a un ser humano	*to kill a human being*

La Dieta

adelgazar — *to lose weight*
el aditivo — *additive*
la anorexia nerviosa — *anorexia nervosa*
los alimentos dietéticos — *health foods*
los alimentos orgánicos — *wholefoods*
el alimento precocinado — *ready-prepared meal*
el almuerzo — *lunch*
el aperitivo — *snack*
el apetito — *appetite*
la bebida — *drink*
la bulimia — *bulimia*
la caloría — *calorie*
el carbohidrato — *carbohydrate*
la cena ligera/pesada — *light/heavy supper*
la clínica de adelgazamiento — *health farm*
la cocina casera — *home cooking*
el colorante artificial — *artificial colouring*
el comestible — *edible*
la comida — *meal*
la comida 'basura' (*inf*) — *junkfood*
el conservante — *preservative*
las conservas — *tinned foods*
crudo — *raw*
desnatado — *skimmed*
el diabético — *diabetic*
la dieta equilibrada — *balanced diet*
la dieta mediterránea — *Mediterranean diet*
la dietética — *dietetics*
el edulcorante — *sweetener*
endulzado — *sweetened*
engordar — *to put on weight*
los entremeses — *hors d'œuvres*
envasado al vacío — *vacuum-packed*
evitar — *to avoid*
la fibra — *fibre*
la gastronomía — *gastronomy*
la golosina — *sweet*
la grasa animal — *animal fat*
la grasa vegetal — *vegetable fat*
el gusto — *taste*
el ingrediente — *ingredient*
la intoxicación alimenticia — *food poisoning*

los lácteos	*milk products*
la leche en polvo	*powdered milk*
la legumbre	*pulse, legume*
la línea	*figure*
el marisco	*seafood, shell fish*
los 'michelines'	*'spare tyre'*
la moderación	*moderation*
nutritivo	*nourishing*
la obesidad	*obesity*
obeso	*obese*
orgánico	*organic*
el pan integral	*wholemeal bread*
perder peso	*to lose weight*
pesarse	*to weigh oneself*
el peso	*weight*
picotear	*nibbling*
el plato	*dish*
el plato combinado	*one-course meal*
el plato principal	*main course*
el postre	*dessert*
el problema de peso	*weight problem*
los productos lácteos	*milk products*
la receta	*recipe*
el régimen	*diet*
el restaurante de comida rápida	*fast-food restaurant*
el sabor	*taste*
la tapa	*snack*
la tienda de alimentación dietética	*health-food shop*
transgénico	*genetically modified*
el valor nutritivo/calorífico	*nutritional/calorific value*
vegetariano	*vegetarian*
la verdura	*vegetables*
la vitamina	*vitamin*

el zumo de frutas es rico en	*fruit juice is rich in*
tener bajo nivel nutritivo	*to have a low nutritional value*
llevar una dieta equilibrada	*to eat a balanced diet*
¡buen provecho!	*enjoy your meal!*
alimentos ricos en fibra	*food rich in fibre*
estar obsesionado por adelgazar	*to be obsessed with slimming*
cuidarse la línea	*to watch one´s figure*
pesar demasiado	*to be overweight*
estar a dieta	*to be on a diet*
disminuir el consumo de	*to cut down on*
picar entre comidas	*to nibble between meals*

La Vida Sana

la alergia *allergy*
el autodiagnóstico *self-diagnosis*
la automedicación *self-medication*
cuidarse *to look after oneself*
diagnosticar *to diagnose*
el diagnóstico precoz *early diagnosis*
el ejercicio regular *regular exercise*
el estrés *stress*
el examen médico *medical examination*
el gimnasio *gym*
la higiene *hygiene*
la higiene dental *dental hygiene*
la hipertensión *high blood-pressure*
hipocondríaco *hypochondriac*
la hipotensión *low blood-pressure*
el infarto *heart attack*
el nivel de azúcar en sangre *blood-sugar level*
el medicamento *medicine*
la prevención *prevention*
los problemas circulatorios *circulation problems*
la relajación *relaxation*
el sistema inmunológico *immune system*
la vacunación *vaccination*
vacunarse contra *to be vaccinated against*

tener la tensión alta/baja *to have high/low blood pressure*
estar/mantenerse en forma *to be/keep fit*
aumentar los niveles de colesterol en tu sangre *to raise cholesterol levels in your blood*
llevar una vida sana *to lead a healthy life*
el chequeo *check up*
más vale prevenir que curar *prevention is better than cure*
ir a un balneario *to go to a spa/health resort*

El Sistema Sanitario Español

el ambulatorio *health centre*
la asistencia médica pública *public health system*
la asistencia pública a domicilio *home-help service*
la asistencia sanitaria *health care*
la clínica privada *private clinic*
el especialista *specialist*

el hospital de la Seguridad Social *Social Security (i.e. NHS) hospital*
la hospitalización *hospitalization*
la lista de espera *waiting list*
las medicinas gratis para los jubilados *free medicines for pensioners*
la medicina general *general practice*
la medicina preventiva *preventive medicine*
el médico de familia *family doctor*
el Ministerio de Salud *Minister of Health*
el pediatra *paediatrician*
la receta *prescription*
recetar *to prescribe*
la rehabilitación *rehabilitation*
la seguridad social *social security*
el seguro privado *private insurance*
urgencias *accident & emergency department*

dar de alta a alguien *to discharge somebody from hospital*
dar de alta a un paciente *to discharge a patient*
Juan está de baja por enfermedad *Juan is off sick*
la estancia hospitalaria *stay in hospital*
la escasez de camas *bed shortage*
debe presentar la baja *you must produce your medical certificate*
fue hospitalizado de urgencia *he was hospitalized as a matter of urgency*

La Medicina Alternativa

la acupuntura *acupuncture*
la aromaterapia *aromatherapy*
la herboristería *herbalist´s*
la hipnosis *hypnosis*
la homeopatía *homeopathy*
el masaje *massage*
la meditación *meditation*
la medicina naturista *naturopathy*
el naturópata *naturopath*
el psicólogo *psychologist*
la reflexología *reflexology*
la relajación *relaxation*
el yoga *yoga*

Los Avances Médicos y La Ética

el ADN *DNA*
el bebé probeta *test-tube baby*
el clon *clone*
la clonación humana *human cloning*
clonar *to clone*
el código ético de conducta *ethical code of conduct*
el donante *donor*
el embrión *embryo*
ético *ethical*
el implante *implant*
el implante electrónico *electronic implant*
inmoral *immoral*
el investigador *researcher*
el gen *gene*
la genética *genetics*
el genoma humano *human genome*
el genotipo *genotype*
la ingeniería genética *genetic engineering*
el lavado de cerebro *brainwashing*
la madre de alquiler *surrogate mother*
el microchip *micro-chip*
los problemas de rechazo *problems of rejection*
el progreso médico *medical progress*
la prótesis *prosthesis*
la robótica *robotics*
el transplante *transplant*

clonar embriones humanos — *to clone human embryos*
identificar el gen de X — *identify the gene for X*
el progreso médico — *medical progress*
la investigación sobre las posibles consecuencias de la manipulación genética — *research into the possible consequences of gene manipulation*
para fines supuestamente científicos — *for supposedly scientific purposes*
la manipulación genética — *gene manipulation*
causar problemas éticos — *to cause ethical problems*

CÓMO AMPLIAR TU VOCABULARIO

Si encuentras la ortografía difícil, prueba el método siguiente:

1 Cuando estés aprendiendo un grupo de palabras pertenecientes a un mismo tema, elige unas 20 o 30 y escríbelas en español y en inglés, pero reemplazando las letras más difíciles de las palabras en español por líneas.

P.ej. *examination* – *rec_ _ _ _ _ _ _ _ _ _ to*
clot – *co_ _ _ _o*

Mira la lista algunos días después y prueba a rellenar los espacios en blanco. Apunta las palabras que no escribas correctamente en tu cuaderno y trata de memorizarlas. Al día siguiente, repite el ejercicio.

Es conveniente repetir el mismo ejercicio a la semana siguiente para fijar definitivamente las palabras en tu memoria.

2 Juega con tu compañero. Escribe una lista de nombres en español; cada palabra deberá tener un error de ortografía.

P.ej. *paziente – patient*

Muestra la lista a tu compañero que deberá tratar de corregir los errores. Cuando tu compañero los haya corregido, le toca a él escribir una lista parecida.

DIRECCIONES ÚTILES EN INTERNET

http://www.medicinainternet.com (información sobre las enfermedades)

http://www.ecomedic.com/em/indice.htm (más de 1000 páginas de salud en español)

http://www.elmedico.net/ (información médica)

http://www.buscasalud.com/ (medicina alternativa, enfermedades, listas de profesionales…)

http://www.ole.es/Paginas/Salud_y_Medicina/ (buscador de Terra, con información sobre clínicas, medicina alternativa, etc)

http://www.rothman.es (página sobre los peligros del tabaco para la salud)

http://www.arrakis.es/iea/kids/6facts.htm (informe sobre los jóvenes y el tabaco)

http://www.msc.es/sida/principal.htm (web sobre el SIDA del Ministerio de Sanidad y Consumo)

http://www.cuidese.net/sida.html (índice de recursos en internet sobre SIDA y VIH)

http://www.medicinatv.es/ (noticias de salud actualizadas)

LOS PROBLEMAS SOCIALES

La Gente Sin Hogar

la caja de cartón	*cardboard box*
desamparado	*helpless, unprotected*
despreciar	*to despise*
la dignidad	*dignity*
gorronear *(inf)*	*to scrounge*
intimidar	*to intimidate*
marginado	*rejected, excluded*
la mendicidad	*begging*
el mendigo	*beggar*
la miseria	*misery*
el músico callejero	*busker*
el ocupante ilegal/el ocupa *(coll)*	*squatter*
pedir	*to beg*
la pérdida del hogar	*loss of home*
la persona desaparecida	*missing person*
la pobreza	*poverty*
proveer de vivienda	*to house*
sobrevivir	*to survive*
la sociedad de consumo	*consumer society*
el vagabundo	*tramp*
la vergüenza	*shame*
vulnerable	*vulnerable*

la gente sin techo	*the homeless*
decadencia de la sociedad	*social decline*
vivir en la miseria	*to live in poverty*
buscar refugio	*to seek refuge*
no tener medios de subsistencia	*to have no means of subsistence*
condiciones de vida insalubres	*insanitary living conditions*
dormir al raso	*to sleep rough*
sin domicilio fijo	*of no fixed abode*
vagar de un lado a otro	*to wander from place to place*
apariencia descuidada	*neglected appearance*
ser rechazado por la sociedad	*to be rejected by society*
fugarse de casa	*to run away from home*
ser echado de tu casa	*to be thrown out of your home*

El Crimen

el abuso a menores *child abuse*
agredir/atacar *to attack*
la agresión *assault*
el agresor *attacker*
el allanamiento de morada *housebreaking*
amenazar *to threaten*
apuñalar *to stab*
armado *armed*
el asesino *murderer*
el atraco *hold-up*
atrapar *to catch*
el chantaje *blackmail*
el criminal *criminal*
dar una paliza *(inf)* *to beat up*
la delincuencia juvenil *juvenile delinquency*
la estafa *swindle*
la evasión fiscal *tax evasion*
el fraude *fraud*
el hurto *shoplifting*
ilegal *illegal*
el incendio provocado *arson*
el índice de criminalidad *crime rate*
el infractor *criminal offender*
el ladrón *thief*
el malhechor *wrong-doer*
la ofensa al pudor *indecent assault*
el pirómano *arsonist*
la prevención del crimen *crime prevention*
el proxeneta *pimp*
el robo *theft*
el robo a mano armada *armed robbery*
secuestrar *to kidnap*
serio *serious*
sobornar *to bribe*
el vandalismo *vandalism*
la víctima *victim*
la violación *rape*
violento *violent*

causar mucho daño *to do a lot of damage*
delincuente juvenil *juvenile delinquent*
alarma antirrobo *burglar alarm*
una banda organizada *an organised gang*
cometer un crimen *to commit a crime*
la lucha contra el crimen *the fight against crime*

El Terrorismo

la amenaza de bomba	*bomb scare*
el artificiero	*bomb expert*
asesinar	*to murder*
el asesinato	*murder*
el asesino	*murderer*
el atentado terrorista	*terrorist outrage*
la bomba	*bomb*
la bomba trampa	*booby-trap bomb*
el coche bomba	*car bomb*
desactivar	*to defuse*
los disturbios	*riots*
ETA (Euskadi Ta Askatasuna)	*ETA (Basque separatist group)*
el etarra	*member of ETA*
la extradición	*extradition*
la granada	*grenade*
el herido	*injured person*
herir	*to injure*
la independencia	*independence*
la masacre	*massacre*
mutilar	*to mutilate*
la organización terrorista	*terrorist organisation*
el rehén	*hostage*
revolucionario	*revolutionary*
sangriento	*bloody*
separatista	*separatist*
el simpatizante	*sympathiser*
el terrorismo	*terrorism*
el terrorista	*terrorist*

un asesinato a sangre fría	*a cold-blooded murder*
desactivar una bomba	*to defuse a bomb*
reivindicar el atentado	*to claim responsibility for the attack*
el efecto devastador de los atentados terroristas	*the devastating effect of terrorist outrages*
la mayoría de las víctimas se eligen por motivos simbólicos	*most of the victims are selected for symbolic reasons*

La Justicia

el abogado	*lawyer, barrister*
absolver	*to acquit*
el acusado	*defendant*
acusar	*to accuse*
arrestar	*to arrest*
las atenuantes	*extenuating circumstances*
atenuar	*to extenuate*
la cadena perpetua	*life imprisonment*
el castigo	*punishment*

condenar	*to convict*
el culpable	*guilty person*
defender	*to defend*
el demandante	*claimant*
demandar	*to sue*
detener	*to detain*
en flagrante delito	*red-handed*
el error judicial	*miscarriage of justice*
inocente	*innocent*
el juez	*judge*
el juicio	*trial*
el jurado	*jury*
la multa	*fine*
la pena capital	*capital punishment*
la pena de muerte	*death penalty*
el perjurio	*perjury*
presunto	*alleged*
el proceso judicial	*legal process*
la prueba	*proof, (piece of) evidence*
el/la reincidente	*reoffender*
el servicio comunitario	*community service*
la sospecha	*suspicion*
el testigo	*witness*
el tribunal	*court*
el tribunal de menores	*juvenile court*
el tribunal supremo	*high court*
la violación de la ley	*breach of the law*

bajo juramento	*on oath*
procesar	*to prosecute*
llevar a alguien a juicio	*to take someone to court*
proceder contra alguien	*to take proceedings against someone*
ganar/perder un caso	*to win/lose a case*
el presunto culpable	*the presumed culprit*
la protesta no procede	*objection overruled*
acusado de tres asesinatos	*charged with three murders*
condenado a dos años de cárcel	*sentenced to two years' imprisonment*
ser condenado injustamente	*to be wrongly convicted*
incriminar a alguien	*to frame someone*
apelar	*to appeal*
suprimir la pena de muerte	*to abolish the death penalty*

La Cárcel

abarrotado	*overcrowded*
los antecedentes penales	*criminal record*
la cárcel	*jail*
el carcelero	*prison officer*
la celda	*cell*
la disciplina	*discipline*
encarcelar	*to imprison*
liberar	*to release, to set free*
la libertad condicional	*probation*
la orden judicial	*warrant*
la penitenciaría	*prison*
el preso preventivo	*remand prisoner*
la prisión de máxima seguridad	*maximum-security prison*
la prisión femenina	*women's prison*
el prisionero	*prisoner*
la reclusión	*confinement*
reformar	*to reform*
la rehabilitación	*rehabilitation*
la reintegración	*reintegration*
el sistema penal	*penal system*

Cómo ampliar tu vocabulario

Cuando aprendas nuevas palabras, agrúpalas haciendo asociaciones. Piensa en una palabra y escríbela, (p.ej. *juicio*). Después, escribe todas las palabras que conozcas que tengan relación con ella, formando un diagrama como éste:

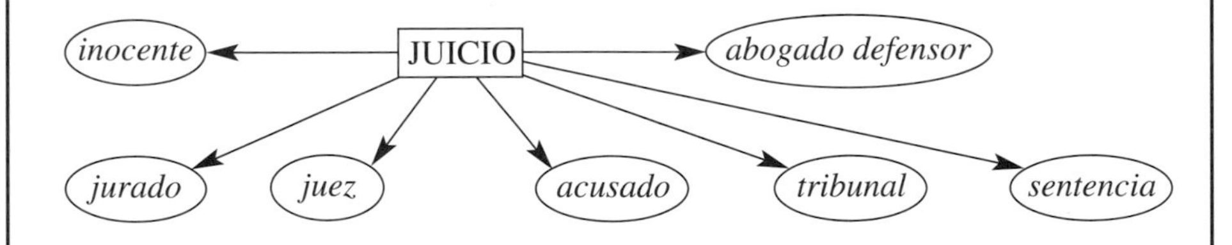

Éste es un ejercicio que se puede hacer individualmente o con los compañeros. Podéis poner un tiempo limitado y hacer una competición con los demás. El que más palabras asociadas consiga en un minuto es el ganador.

Direcciones útiles en Internet

http://www.ncpc.org/espanol.htm (la prevención del crimen)

http://www.derechos.org/esp.html (los derechos humanos)

http://www.terra.es/actualidad/terrorismo (el terrorismo en España)

http://www.mju.es (web oficial del Ministerio de Justicia)

LA ECONOMÍA

El Comercio

arriesgado	*risky*
arriesgar	*to risk*
la asociación	*partnership*
los beneficios	*profits*
los bienes	*goods*
la Cámara de Comercio	*Chamber of Commerce*
la carta comercial	*business letter*
la clientela	*customers*
la compra	*purchase*
la compañía	*firm*
el consumidor	*consumer*
el consumismo	*consumerism*
la contabilidad	*accounting*
el descuento	*reduction*
la exportación	*export*
la factura	*bill*
la filial	*subsidiary office*
la gama de productos	*product range*
la globalización	*globalisation*
la guerra de precios	*price war*
la importación	*import*
importar	*to import*
el margen de beneficio	*profit margin*
el mayorista	*wholesaler*
el mercado de telecomunicaciones	*telecommunications market*
la mercancía	*merchandise*
el minorista	*retailer*
el monopolio	*monopoly*
la oferta y la demanda	*supply and demand*
las pérdidas	*losses*
el poder adquisitivo	*purchasing power*
el producto	*product*
la promoción	*special offer*
las rebajas	*sales*
la reclamación	*complaint*
reembolsar	*to refund*
la rentabilidad	*profitability*
repartir	*to deliver*
el riesgo	*risk*
la venta a plazos	*hire purchase*
la venta al contado	*cash sale*
la venta al por mayor	*wholesale*
la venta al por menor	*retail sale*

aumentar/bajar los precios	*to increase/lower prices*
el reparto a domicilio	*home delivery service*
responder a las necesidades de los clientes	*to meet the customers' needs*
la oferta y la demanda	*supply and demand*
ser un negocio rentable	*to be a profitable business*

importaron bienes por valor de	*they imported goods to a value of*
poner algo a la venta	*to put something on sale*
hacer recortes	*to make cutbacks*
ir a la bancarrota	*to go bankrupt*

La Banca

ahorrar	*to save*
la banca	*the banks, banking*
el banco	*bank*
bruto	*gross*
la caja de ahorros	*savings bank*
el cajero	*cash point*
el cambio	*exchange*
la carta de crédito	*credit card*
el cheque	*cheque*
el crédito	*credit*
la cuenta corriente	*current account*
la cuenta de ahorro	*savings account*
el depósito	*deposit*
las divisas	*foreign currency*
la hipoteca	*mortgage*
hipotecar	*to mortgage*
insolvente	*insolvent*
la inversión	*investment*
el interés	*interest*
neto	*net*
el número secreto	*PIN number*
el préstamo	*loan*
prestar	*to lend*
retirar	*to withdraw*
el saldo deudor	*overdraft*
el sector bancario	*banking industry*
solvente	*solvent*
la sucursal	*branch*
la tarjeta de crédito	*credit card*
los tipos de interés	*interest rate*
la transacción	*transaction*

cobrar un cheque	*to cash a cheque*
ingresar dinero en una cuenta	*to pay money into an account*
estar en números rojos	*to be in the red*
domiciliar una cuenta	*to debit an account directly*
descuento por pago al contado	*cash discount*
pedir un préstamo	*to ask for a loan*
abrir/cerrar una cuenta	*to open/close an account*
el saldo de una cuenta	*the account balance*
pagar en metálico	*to pay by cash*
hacer una transferencia	*to transfer*

LAS FINANZAS

la acción	*share*
el accionista	*shareholder*
el agente de Bolsa	*stockbroker*
el año fiscal	*tax year*
la bancarrota	*bankruptcy*
el billón	*billion*
la Bolsa	*Stock Exchange*
el capital	*capital*
la carga fiscal	*tax burden*
el contribuyente	*taxpayer*
la crisis	*crisis*
la deuda nacional	*the national debt*
la deuda pública	*national debt*
endeudarse	*to get into debt*
especular	*to speculate*
el euro	*euro*
la factura	*invoice*
facturar	*to invoice*
financiar	*to finance*
el fraude fiscal	*tax evasion*
el gasto	*expenditure*
el impuesto sobre la renta	*income tax*
la inflación	*inflation*
insolvente	*insolvent*
la inversión	*investment*
el inversor	*investor*
IVA (el impuesto sobre el valor añadido)	*VAT (value added tax)*
el libre mercado	*free-trade*
el millón	*million*
la nacionalización	*nationalisation*
nacionalizar	*to nationalise*
las perspectivas	*prospects*
el porcentaje	*percentage*
el presupuesto	*budget*
la privatización	*privatisation*
privatizar	*to privatise*
la recesión	*recession*
el recibo	*receipt*
solvente	*solvent*
la subida de los precios	*price rise*

subir los impuestos	*to raise taxes*
invertir en acciones	*to invest in shares*
la devaluación/revaluación de la peseta	*the devaluation/revaluation of the peseta*
la tasa de inflación	*inflation rate*
el déficit exterior es muy alto	*the balance of payments deficit is very high*
declararse en bancarrota	*to go bankrupt*
la balanza de pagos	*the balance of payments*
favorecer el crecimiento económico	*to encourage economic growth*
el poder adquisitivo	*purchasing power*

La Industria

el accidente laboral *industrial accident*
el acuerdo *agreement*
el comité de empresa *works committee*
la competitividad *competitiveness*
competitivo *competitive*
las condiciones de trabajo *working conditions*
el convenio colectivo *collective agreement*
la cooperativa *co-operative*
la cooperativa agrícola *farming co-operative*
la dirección *management*
la empresa de servicios públicos *public utility company*
la empresa filial *subsidiary company*
la empresa pública/privada *public/private sector company*
el empresario *businessman*
la empresa transnacional *multinational company*
el envasado *packing*
la fábrica *factory*
la fabricación *manufacture*
la formación *training*
la fusión de las grandes compañías *merger of big companies*
el gerente *manager*
las horas laborables *business hours*
la huelga *strike*
incrementar la productividad *to increase productivity*
el índice de siniestralidad *accident rate*
la industria artesanal *cottage industry*
la industria de alta tecnología *high-tech industry*
la industria del automóvil *car industry*
la industria manufacturera *manufacturing industry*
la industria pesquera *fishing industry*
la industria siderúrgica *iron and steel industry*
la industria terciaria *service industry*
la industria textil *textile industry*
el industrialismo *industrialism*
las innovaciones técnicas *technical innovations*
la inversión *investment*
la junta de accionistas *shareholders' meeting*
la materia prima *commodity*
el medio ambiente *environment*
las negociaciones *negotiations*
el operario de la máquina *the machine operator*
las organizaciones empresariales *the employers' organisations*
la patronal *management*
las pérdidas *losses*
el polígono industrial *industrial estate*
los procesos industriales avanzados *advanced industrial processes*

producir *to produce*
la productividad *productivity*
los productos manufacturados *manufactured goods*
la regulación *regulation*
la reivindicación *claim*
el robot *robot*
el salario mínimo *minimum wage*
la sanción *fine*
la subcontratación *subcontracting*
el volumen de ventas *volume of sales*
el sector *sector*
la tecnología *technology*
el trabajo en cadena *work on a production line*
sociedad anónima (S.A.) *public limited company (plc)*
sociedad limitada (S.L.) *limited company (Co. Ltd.)*

Cómo ampliar tu vocabulario

Otro juego para ampliar tu conocimiento de vocabulario: el juego de la *escalera*. Juega con tu compañero/a o en grupo. Escoged una letra. Cada jugador tiene que ir construyendo la *escalera*. El jugador que construya la escalera más larga en cinco minutos es el que gana.

P.ej: 1 *s* 5 *sello*
2 *su* 6 *suelto*
3 *sol* 7 *soltero*
4 *sofá* ....

Apunta las palabras nuevas que digan otros compañeros en tu cuaderno de vocabulario.

Direcciones útiles en Internet

http://www.netgocio.com/ (finanzas, trabajo, telecomunicaciones, etc)

http://www.economyweb.com/ (una de las páginas más completas de economía en español)

http://www.consejero.com/ (información económica sobre América Latina)

http://www.megabolsa.com/ (página de finanzas y mercados de la bolsa en español)

http://www.nueva-economia.com (revista electrónica de economía del diario "El Mundo")

http://www.spaindustry.com (directorio multimedia de la industria española)

http://www.e-global.es (web general sobre el comercio electrónico)

LA TECNOLOGÍA DE LA INFORMACIÓN Y LA INVESTIGACIÓN CIENTÍFICA

Hardware

el accesorio *accessory*
la agenda electrónica *electronic organiser*
el CD-ROM *CD-ROM*
el chip *computer chip*
el circuito *circuit*
el disco duro *hard disk*
el disquete *floppy disk*
el escáner *scanner*
la impresora de color *colour printer*
la impresora láser *laser printer*
el módem *modem*
el monitor *monitor*
el ordenador *computer*
el ordenador de uso doméstico *home computer*
el ordenador 'notebook' *notebook computer*
el ordenador personal *PC*
la pantalla *screen*
portátil *portable*
el ratón ergonómico *ergonomic mouse*
recargar la batería *to recharge the battery*
la red *network*
el salvapantallas *screen saver*
los servicios informáticos *computer services*
el servidor *server*
el teclado *keyboard*
el teléfono WAP *WAP phone*
el terminal *terminal*
la unidad de disco *disk drive*
la unidad de proceso *mainframe*

Software

la actualización *update*
el almacenamiento de datos *data storage*
almacenar *to store*
la animación *animation*
la ayuda *help*
la base de datos *database*
la capacidad de memoria *memory size*
compatible *compatible*

el documento *document*
DOS (sistema operativo de disco) *DOS*
el fichero de datos *data file*
funcional *functional*
la funcionalidad *functionality*
la hoja de cálculo *spreadsheet*
el intercambio de datos *data exchange*
el lenguaje de programación *programming language*
la memoria de programa *program memory*
el menú *menu*
multimedia *multimedia*
el procesador de textos *word-processor*
procesar *to process*
el programa *program*
el programador *programmer*
programar *to program*
el sistema auxiliar *back-up system*
el sonido *sound*
el tratamiento de textos *word-processing*
la ventana de diálogo *pop-up window*
el virus informático *computer virus*

a través de mejoras tecnológicas *through technological improvements*
aprendizaje asistido por ordenador *computer-assisted learning*
la revolución informática *the information-technology revolution*
la era de la informática *the computer age*

Las Funciones

actualizar *to update*
archivar *to save*
cancelar *to cancel*
cargar *to load*
conectar *to connect*
copiar *to copy*
cortar *to cut*
diseñar *to design*
editar *to edit*
entrar/salir del sistema *to log on/off*
escanear *to scan*
formatear *to format*
imprimir *to print out*
insertar *to insert*
introducir (datos) *to enter (data)*
pegar *to paste*
personalizar *to personalise*
recuperar *to retrieve*
transmitir *to transmit*
visualizar *to display*

diseñar una página web	*to design a website*
conectarse a internet	*to connect to the internet*
intercambiar información con gente de todo el mundo	*to exchange information with people around the world*
escanear fotografías	*to scan pictures*
instalar nuevos programas informáticos	*to install new computer programs*

INTERNET

el buzón de correo	*mailbox*
el chat	*chat room*
chatear	*to chat*
el cibercafé	*cybercafé*
el ciberespacio	*cyberspace*
la conexión a internet	*internet connection*
la contraseña	*password*
la contraseña de usuario	*user password*
la descarga	*download*
descargar	*to download*
la dirección de correo electrónico	*e-mail address*
el doble clic	*double click*
el dominio	*domain*
el dominio protegido	*protected domain*
empezar una búsqueda	*to start a search*
el enlace	*link*
el foro	*forum*
el identificador de usuario	*user ID*
el internauta	*web surfer*
en línea	*on line*
el motor de búsqueda	*search engine*
el navegador	*web browser*
navegar en la web	*to surf the web*
las opciones	*options*
el portal	*portal*
el proveedor	*provider*
el punto	*dot*
la realidad virtual	*virtual reality*
el sitio web	*website*
la tecnología de la información	*information technology*
el URL (localizador uniforme de recursos)	*URL*
el usuario	*user*

todo se hará a través del ordenador	*everything will be done by computer*
hacer clic en un enlace	*to click on a link*
actualizar una página web	*to update a webpage*
usando un teléfono WAP, puedes tener acceso constante a las noticias	*using a WAP phone, you have constant access to news*

Los Problemas

el programa antivirus — *antivirus program*
el adicto a la red — *web addict*
la censura — *censorship*
la compatibilidad — *compatibility*
la copia pirata — *pirate copy*
el disquete contaminado — *corrupted disk*
el error del sistema — *system error*
la factura telefónica — *phone bill*
frustrante — *frustrating*
el pirata informático/el hacker — *hacker*
la piratería del software — *software piracy*
la pornografía dura/blanda — *hard/soft pornography*
la seguridad de la base de datos — *database security*
el uso de internet — *use of the internet*
el virus — *virus*

los niños corren el peligro de convertirse en adictos del ordenador — *children are in danger of becoming computer addicts*
está siempre con el ordenador — *he/she is always on the computer*
introdujeron un virus — *they introduced a virus*

La Investigación Científica

adaptarse — *to adapt*
el astronauta — *astronaut*
los avances tecnológicos — *technological advances*
el bienestar — *welfare*
la biología — *biology*
el biólogo — *biologist*
la ciencia — *science*
el científico — *scientist*
el cohete — *rocket*
desarrollar — *to develop*
el equipo — *equipment*
la estación espacial — *space station*
experimentar — *to experiment*
el experimento — *experiment*
la física — *physics*
el físico — *physicist*
la genética — *genetics*
la ingravidez — *weightlessness*
el investigador — *researcher*
investigar — *to research*
el laboratorio — *laboratory*
lanzar — *to launch*
la misión espacial — *space mission*
la NASA — *NASA*

el proceso	*process*
la química	*chemistry*
el químico	*chemist*
los resultados	*results*
el robot	*robot*
el satélite	*satellite*
la sustancia	*substance*
la tecnología	*technology*
el transbordador espacial	*space shuttle*
la tripulación	*crew*

la alta tecnología/tecnología punta	*high technology*
vivimos en una sociedad desarrollada	*we live in a developed society*
promover la investigación científica	*to promote scientific research*
poner un satélite en órbita	*to put a satellite into orbit*
formas de vida extraterrestre	*extraterrestrial life forms*
misión humana a Marte	*human mission to Mars*
llevar a cabo experimentos	*to carry out experiments*
comunicaciones via satélite	*satellite communications*
la exploración del espacio	*space exploration*
beneficiarse de los avances científicos	*to benefit from scientific advances*

Cómo ampliar tu vocabulario

Aprovecha la tecnología para aprender nuevas palabras. Graba en un cassette las palabras y frases que encuentres útiles para tratar de un tema determinado. Primero léelas en español, deja una pausa y tradúcelas al inglés. Finalmente, dejando otra pausa, repítelas en español.

P.ej: *tecnología – technology – tecnología*

Escucha la grabación varias veces e intenta decir la palabra en español durante la segunda pausa. De esta forma practicas la pronunciación y fijas el significado en tu mente.

Direcciones útiles en Internet

http://www.ciencianet.com (la ciencia vista de una forma divertida)

http://www.solarviews.com/span/homepage/htm (nuestro sistema solar)

http://www.optize.es (ofertas especiales de hardware y sofware, glosario de términos informáticos, etc.)

http://www.ciberpais.elpais.es/ (Suplemento del diario 'El País' dedicado al mundo de la informática)

LOS MEDIOS DE COMUNICACIÓN

El Transporte

el accidente *accident*
aparcar *to park*
el atasco *traffic jam*
aterrizar *to land*
el autobús *bus, coach*
el/la automovilista *motorist*
la autopista *motorway*
la autopista de peaje *toll motorway*
la autovía *dual carriageway*
la calzada *roadway*
la carretera de peaje *toll road*
el carril para bicicletas *cycle lane*
el cinturón de seguridad *seatbelt*
conducir *to drive*
el cruce a distinto nivel *motorway junction (on a different level)*
el cruce al mismo nivel *motorway junction (on same level)*
despegar *to take off (a plane)*
desplazarse *to travel*
facturar el equipaje *to check in*
la gasolina *petrol*
la hora punta *rush hour*
el límite de velocidad *speed limit*
la línea aérea *airline*
modernizar *to modernize*
el peaje *toll*
el permiso de conducir *driving licence*
la red de carreteras *road network*
la RENFE (Red Nacional de los Ferrocarriles Españoles) *Spanish Railways*
los servicios de cercanías *commuter services*
la seguridad *security*
el tráfico *traffic*
el transporte aéreo *air transport*
el tren de alta velocidad *high-speed train*
la velocidad *speed*
el volumen de tráfico *volume of traffic*
el vuelo chárter *charter flight*
el vuelo regular *scheduled flight*
la zona peatonal *pedestrian precinct*

el uso del transporte público *the use of public transport*
planificar la red de carreteras *to plan the road network*
invertir en la infraestructura *to invest in the infrastructure*
una catástrofe debida a un fallo mecánico *a disaster caused by a mechanical fault*

acortar las distancias	*to reduce the distances*
modernizar los servicios de transporte	*to modernize the transport services*
el avión de pasajeros	*passenger aircraft*
el Ministerio de Transportes	*Ministry of Transport*
el parque nacional de automóviles	*the total number of cars in the country*
evitar la formación de excesivo tráfico	*not to allow excess traffic to build up*
fomentar el uso del transporte público	*to encourage people to use public transport*

La Televisión

la antena	*aerial*
la antena parabólica	*satellite dish*
el anuncio	*advertisement*
la audiencia	*audience*
borroso	*blurred*
la cadena	*channel*
la 'caja tonta' *(inf)*	*goggle-box*
la calidad de imagen	*picture quality*
el canal de televisión	*television channel*
captar	*to receive*
censurar	*to censor*
el concurso	*competition, contest*
el contraste	*contrast*
el control remoto	*remote control*
el corresponsal en el extranjero	*foreign correspondent*
el decodificador	*decoder*
el documental	*documentary*
el DVD	*DVD*
la emisión	*broadcast*
la emisión deportiva	*sports programme*
emitir	*to broadcast*
encender/apagar	*to switch on/off*
el episodio	*episode*
el equipo de filmación	*camera crew*
el formato digital	*digital format*
grabar en vídeo	*to record, to video*
la hora de emisión	*broadcast time*
la hora de máxima audiencia	*peak-viewing time*
la interferencia	*disturbance*
la interrupción	*interruption*
el invitado	*guest*
el lector de DVD	*DVD player*
local	*local*
el locutor	*announcer*
el locutor de telediario	*newscaster*
los medios de comunicación	*mass media*
el mercado del vídeo	*video market*
las noticias	*news*
las noticias de última hora	*newsflash*
la pantalla	*screen*
la película	*film*

la pequeña pantalla *the small screen*
el programa de tertulia *chat show*
la programación *programme planning*
el promotor *promoter*
la recepción *reception*
la red *network*
regional *regional*
la reposición *repeat*
salir en televisión *to be on television*
la serie televisiva *television series*
la tecnología de satélite *satellite technology*
la tele *(inf)* *telly*
teleadicto *addicted to television*
el telediario *television news bulletin*
la telenovela *soap opera*
el telespectador *TV viewer*
el teletexto *teletext*
la televisión digital *digital TV*
la televisión en blanco y negro *black and white TV*
la televisión en color *colour TV*
la televisión interactiva *interactive television*
la televisión matinal *breakfast television*
la televisión por cable *cable television*
la televisión por satélite *satellite television*
la transmisión en diferido *recorded transmission*
la transmisión en directo *live transmission*
transmitir *to transmit*
transmitir en directo *to broadcast live*
vía satélite *via satellite*

el canal de televisión local	*local TV channel*
una ventana abierta al mundo	*a(n open) window on the world*
la televisión difunde cultura	*television propagates culture*
traer el mundo a tu hogar	*to bring the world into your home*
llegar a todos	*to reach everyone*
con subtítulos para aquéllos con problemas de audición	*with subtitles for the hard of hearing*
programas habituales	*regular programmes*
X es un canal privado	*X is a private channel*
quedarse pegado al televisor	*to be glued to the television*
sentarse delante de la caja tonta *(inf)*	*to sit in front of the box*
cambiar a otro canal	*to switch over to another channel*
la presentadora es Isabel Gemio	*the presenter is Isabel Gemio*

La Radio

la banda de frecuencias *waveband*
la calidad de sonido *sound quality*
la comedia radiofónica *radio play*
la emisión de radio *radio broadcast*
la emisora de radio *radio station*
emitir *to broadcast*
el entrevistador *interviewer*
estéreo *stereo*
la frecuencia *frequency*
la información sobre el tráfico *traffic report*
el locutor de radio *announcer*
la longitud de onda *wavelength*
el micrófono *microphone*
la onda *wave*
el oyente *listener*
el pinchadiscos/disc-jockey *disc jockey*
el presentador *presenter*
el programa radiofónico *radio programme*
la radio *radio*
la radio pirata *pirate radio station*
la radiodifusión *broadcasting*

sintonizar la Cadena Ser *to tune into Cadena Ser*
programa regional *regional programme*
en directo desde el estudio *live from the studio*

La Prensa

el anuncio *announcement*
los archivos *archives*
el articulista *feature-writer*
el artículo *article*
el artículo de fondo *editorial article*
la calumnia *libel*
la columna *column*
el comentario *commentary*
el comunicado de prensa *press release*
la conferencia de prensa *press conference*
la contribución *contribution*
el corresponsal *correspondent*
la crónica de sociedad *gossip column*
la crónica literaria *literary page*
demandar *to sue*
los derechos de autor *copyright*
el diario *daily paper*
difamatorio *libellous*
la difusión *circulation*
la documentación *documentation*
el editor *publisher*
el editorial *editorial (article)*
el ejemplar *copy*
el equipo de redacción *editorial team*
la errata *misprint*

la exclusiva	*exclusive*
ilustrado	*illustrated*
imprimir	*to print*
la investigación	*investigation*
la libertad de prensa	*freedom of the press*
mensualmente	*monthly*
la noticia	*news item*
el número de lectores	*readership*
el periodismo	*journalism*
el/la periodista	*journalist*
la prensa sensacionalista	*gutter press*
la primicia informativa	*scoop*
la redacción	*editorial staff*
el redactor jefe	*editor-in-chief*
el reportaje	*report*
el reportero	*reporter*
la revista	*magazine*
la revista del corazón	*glossy magazine*
la rueda de prensa	*press conference*
la sección de contactos	*personal column*
la sección deportiva	*sports section*
la sección económica	*financial pages*
el semanario	*weekly paper*
la subscripción	*subscription*
el subscriptor	*subscriber*
el suplemento	*supplement*
el tabloide	*tabloid*
la tirada	*print run*
el titular	*headline*

tener informado al lector	*to keep the reader informed*
garantizar la libertad de expresión	*to guarantee free speech*
la prensa sensacionalista	*the gutter press*
un periódico de calidad	*a quality newspaper*
subscribirse a un periódico	*to subscribe to a newspaper*
según fuentes bien informadas	*according to well-informed sources*
ser noticia de primera plana	*to hit the headlines*
el deber público de la prensa	*the public duty of the press*
información objetiva	*objective reporting*
la revista de modas	*fashion magazine*
pornografía dura/blanda	*hard/soft porn*
entrometerse en la vida privada de alguien	*to intrude on someone's privacy*
las leyes contra la difamación	*libel laws*
un juicio parcial	*biased judgement*
apoyar una opinión política	*to support a political opinion*

La Publicidad

la agencia de publicidad *advertising agency*
el anunciante *advertiser*
el anuncio clasificado *classified advert*
el anuncio publicitario *advert*
la campaña de ventas *sales campaign*
la campaña publicitaria *advertising campaign*
la cartelera *hoarding, billboard*
el consumidor *consumer*
convencer *to convince*
deformar la realidad *to distort the truth*
engañoso *deceitful*
el eslogan *slogan*
incrementar las ventas *to increase sales*
el intermedio *commercial break*
la libertad de expresión *freedom of speech*
la marca *brand*
la muestra gratuita *free sample*
patrocinar *to sponsor*
persuadir *to persuade*
el póster *poster*
los productos de marca *branded goods*
promocionar *to promote*
la valla publicitaria *hoarding, billboard*

influencia la vida de millones	*it influences the lives of millions*
tener un efecto en alguien	*to have an effect on someone*
X influencia la vida de los jóvenes	*young people's lives are influenced by X*
el lavado de cerebro	*brainwashing*
vivimos en una sociedad de consumo	*we live in a consumer society*
X se financia a través de la publicidad	*X is dependent on advertising*
perjudicial para los jóvenes	*harmful to young people*
dejarse manipular por	*to let oneself be manipulated by*
te incita a gastar dinero	*it encourages you to spend money*
el estudio de mercado	*market survey*

GENERAL

la actitud	*attitude*
anunciar	*to announce*
el censor	*censor*
la censura	*censorship*
comunicar	*to convey*
la desinformación	*disinformation*
educativo	*educational*
efectivo	*effective*
el entendimiento	*understanding*
la era multimedia	*multimedia age*
expresarse	*to express oneself*
incitar	*to incite*
influenciar	*to influence*
informar	*to inform*
los medios de comunicación de masas	*mass media*
objetivo	*objective*
parcial	*one-sided*
la pornografía	*pornography*
pornográfico	*pornographic*
propagar	*to disseminate*
la propaganda	*propaganda*
el subconsciente	*sub-consciousness*
los temas de actualidad	*current affairs*
la transmisión	*transmission*

CÓMO AMPLIAR TU VOCABULARIO

Cuando estés aprendiendo un nuevo grupo de palabras, puedes crear tus propios juegos:

Elije una palabra de muchas letras (p.ej. *periodismo)* y trata de formar cuantas palabras puedas usando sus letras, p.ej.

período, medio, medir, odio, oído, pero, oír, río, dios, oro, ...

Puedes hacerlo tú solo (es un buen ejercicio) o concursar con más compañeros (el ganador puede ser el que más palabras consiga o el que consiga la palabra más larga).

¡Y acuérdate de anotar en tu cuaderno de vocabulario las palabras que otros digan y que son nuevas para ti!

DIRECCIONES ÚTILES EN INTERNET

http://www.elpais.es (el diario más leído de España)

http://www.marca.es/ (acceso al diario deportivo 'Marca')

http://www.europapress.es (agencia española de noticias)

http://www.rtve.es/tve/index.html (página de la televisión española)

— EL MEDIO AMBIENTE —

TIPOS DE ENERGÍA

el acumulador *storage battery*
los adelantos técnicos *technical advances*
los aerogeneradores *wind turbine*
agotar *to exhaust*
ahorrar energía *to save energy*
el carbón *coal*
la central eléctrica *power station*
la central nuclear *nuclear power station*
los combustibles fósiles *fossil fuels*
el consumo de energía *energy consumption*
el desecho radioactivo *radioactive waste*
la energía alternativa *alternative energy*
la energía eólica *wind energy*
la energía geotérmica *geothermal energy*
la energía hidraúlica *water power*
la energía nuclear *nuclear energy*
la energía renovable/no renovable *renewable/finite energy*
la energía solar *solar energy*
la fusión nuclear *nuclear fusion*
el gas natural *natural gas*
el oleoducto *oil pipeline*
el parque eólico *wind farm*
la placa solar *solar panel*
la plataforma petrolífera *oil platform*
el pozo de petróleo *oil well*
la prueba nuclear *nuclear test*
radioactivo *radioactive*
el reactor nuclear *nuclear reactor*
los vertidos nucleares *nuclear waste*
los yacimientos de petróleo *oil deposits*

estar en contra del uso de la energía nuclear *to be against the use of nuclear energy*
el desperdicio de nuestros recursos *the wastage of our resources*
el consumo de recursos naturales *the consumption of natural resources*
la crisis del petróleo *the oil crisis*
una política de conservación *a conservation policy*
las reservas sin explotar *unexploited reserves*
buscar recursos energéticos alternativos *to look for alternative sources of energy*

LA CONTAMINACIÓN

el agujero en la capa de ozono *hole in the ozone layer*
alarmante *alarming*
los cambios en el ecosistema *changes in the ecosystem*
el clima *climate*
la contaminación acústica *noise pollution*
la contaminación de las aguas *water pollution*
el contaminante *pollutant*
contaminar *to pollute*
dañar *to damage*
el daño al mundo animal *damage to the animal world*
el desastre ecológico *environmental disaster*
desconsiderado *inconsiderate*
descontaminar *to decontaminate*
los desechos tóxicos *toxic waste*
la desertización *(process of) turning into a desert*
el deterioro ambiental *environmental damage*
la ecología *ecology*
ecológico *ecological*
el ecologista *ecologist*
el ecosistema *ecosystem*
el efecto invernadero *greenhouse effect*
las emisiones *emissions*
la energía solar *solar power*
envenenado *poisoned*
envenenar *to poison*
el equilibrio ecológico *ecological balance*
evitar *to avoid*
la extinción *extinction*
la gasolina sin plomo *unleaded petrol*
la insonorización *soundproofing*
irreversible *irreversible*
la lluvia ácida *acid rain*
la marea negra *oil spill*
malgastar *to waste*
el medio ambiente *environment*
el Ministerio del Medio Ambiente *Department of the Environment*
el movimiento ecologista *ecology movement*
la niebla tóxica *smog*
los niveles de ozono *ozone levels*
el nivel sonoro máximo *maximun noise level*
peligroso para la salud *dangerous to health*
el petróleo *crude oil*
la política energética *energy policy*
la polución *pollution*
la polución atmosférica *air pollution*
la preocupación ambiental *environmental concern*

el producto ecológico *environmentally-friendly product*
el producto orgánico *organically-grown product*
la protección *protection*
proteger *to protect*
las radiaciones ultravioletas *ultraviolet radiation*
el recalentamiento del planeta *global warming*
los recursos naturales *natural resources*
la reducción *reduction*
reemplazar *to replace*
salvaguardar *to safeguard*
salvar *to save*
la selva tropical *rain forest*
el sistema ecológico *ecological system*
la supervivencia *survival*
tóxico *poisonous*
los trastornos auditivos *hearing disorders*

la limpieza de las playas	*cleaning up the beaches*
dañino para el medio ambiente	*harmful to the environment*
el nivel del mar está subiendo	*the sea-level is rising*
un peligro para la salud	*a health hazard*
cambios en el ecosistema	*changes in the ecosystem*
la destrucción de la capa de ozono	*destruction of the ozone layer*
la destrucción de la selva tropical	*destruction of the rain forest*
causar daños irreversibles	*to cause irreversible damage*
medir las consecuencias	*to measure the consequences*

Los Elementos Contaminantes

el aerosol *aerosol*
el aire acondicionado *air conditioner*
la bolsa de plástico *plastic bag*
el cloro *chlorine*
el clorofluorocarbono *CFC (chlorofluorocarbon)*
los combustibles fósiles *fossil fuels*
el consumo de energía *energy consumption*
el contaminante *pollutant*
deforestar *to deforest*
el desecho tóxico *toxic waste*
despilfarrar *to squander*
el dióxido de carbono *carbon dioxide*

los envases de cartón *cardboard packaging*
el fertilizante *fertiliser*
el fosfato *phosphate*
los gases contaminantes *polluting gases*
la gasolina con plomo *leaded petrol*
los hidrocarburos *hydrocarbons*
la mancha de petróleo *(small) oil slick*
la marea negra *oil spill, (large) oil slick*
el mercurio *mercury*
el metano *methane*
el nitrógeno *nitrogen*
el oxígeno *oxygen*
el pesticida *pesticide*
el poliestireno *polystyrene*
el reciclaje *recycling*
los residuos radioactivos *radioactive waste*
la sociedad consumista *consumer society*
el spray *spray*
el tubo de escape *exhaust pipe*

las sustancias que dañan la capa de ozono *substances which harm the ozone layer*
la amenaza al equilibrio ecológico *the threat to the ecological balance*
un producto que no daña el medio ambiente *an environmentally-friendly product*
los temas ecológicos *the green issues*
usar una crema que proteja contra los rayos ultravioleta (UV) *to use a cream which protects against ultraviolet (UV) rays*
hacer que la gente se conciencie *to raise people's consciousness*
dañar el medio ambiente *to damage the environment*
la lluvia torrencial *torrential rain*

La Eliminación del Material de Desecho

el abono orgánico *organic fertiliser*
el abono químico *chemical fertiliser*
la basura *rubbish*
el contenedor *container*
el contenedor de vidrio *bottle bank*
el cubo de la basura *dustbin*
la depuradora de aguas residuales *sewage treatment plant*
el desecho biológico *biological waste*
los desechos industriales *industrial waste*
los desperdicios *waste products*
el envase de vidrio *glass container*

el envase no retornable *non-returnable empty*
el envase retornable *returnable empty*
la incineración *incineration*
el incinerador *incinerator*
el material sintético *synthetic material*
el papel reciclado *recycled paper*
el papel usado *waste paper*
el reciclaje *recycling*
reciclar *to recycle*
la recogida de basuras *rubbish collection*
reutilizable *reusable*
reutilizar *to reuse*
el triturador de basuras *waste disposal unit*
el vertedero *rubbish dump*
verter *to dump*

los materiales reciclables van en el contenedor verde — *recyclable materials go in the green dustbin*
aumentar el uso de los envases retornables — *to increase the use of returnable empties*
los incineradores producen problemas de contaminación — *incinerators produce pollution problems*
clasificar la basura — *to sort the rubbish*
los materiales no reciclables van en el contenedor azul — *non-recyclable materials go in the blue dustbin*

Los Derechos De Los Animales

la amenaza a la naturaleza *the threat to wildlife*
anestesiar *to anaesthetise*
atroz *atrocious*
la biodiversidad *biodiversity*
el cambio climático *climate change*
la caza *hunting*
la caza de ballenas/focas *whale/seal hunting*
el cazador furtivo *poacher*
el cobayo *(fig)* *guinea pig*
el conejillo de indias *guinea pig*
la corrida de toros *bull fighting*
criar *to breed*
la crueldad *cruelty*
dañar *to damage*
la desertización *turning land into desert*
domar *to tame*
entrenar *to train*
envenenar *to poison*
la especie amenazada *endangered species*
el experimento *experiment*

la extinción *extinction*
la fauna *wildlife*
la foca *seal*
la investigación médica *medical investigation*
la lluvia torrencial *torrential rain*
el matadero *slaughterhouse*
modificar el ecosistema *to change the ecosystem*
el movimiento ecologista *ecology movement*

prohibir *to ban*
la protección de la naturaleza *nature protection*
la selva tropical *rainforest*
sentir pena por *to feel pity for*
el sufrimiento *suffering*
la supervivencia de las especies *the survival of the species*
la tala *felling*
verter al mar *to tip into the sea*
la vivisección *vivisection*

el comercio ilegal de marfil	*the illegal trade in ivory*
el defensor de los derechos de los animales	*animal rights activist*
estar a favor de la prohibición de	*to be in favour of a ban on*
estar en contra de la exportación de ganado	*to be against the exportation of livestock*
paradas cada ocho horas cuando se transporta ganado	*rest periods every eight hours when transporting livestock*
la crueldad con los animales	*cruelty to animals*
estar en peligro de extinción	*to be endangered*
amenazar el equilibrio ecológico	*to threaten the ecological balance*
causar daños irreversibles	*to cause irreversible damage*
la destrucción de los bosques	*destruction of forests*
el movimiento pro derechos de los animales	*animal rights movement*

Cómo ampliar tu vocabulario

Para ampliar tu conocimiento de vocabulario prueba este juego:

Juega con varios compañeros. Limitad el vocabulario a un campo semántico, p.ej. *El medio ambiente.* El primer jugador comienza diciendo: *Ayer me encontré un/a...* y añade un nombre, p.ej. *fertilizante.* El siguiente deberá repetir la frase, pero añadiendo otra palabra más, de forma que la lista se va haciendo cada vez más larga.

El jugador que cometa un error queda eliminado. El siguiente comienza otra vez. El juego termina cuando sólo quede un jugador.

Puedes hacerlo más difícil todavía haciendo que cada jugador diga un nombre acompañado de un adjetivo, p.ej. *gas contaminante, lluvia ácida, ...* .

Direcciones útiles en Internet

http://www.ecoportal.com.ar/ (portal argentino de recursos sobre ecología y medio ambiente)

http://www.guiaverde.com/arboles/principa.htm (página descriptiva de las principales especies de árboles de España)

http://www.icb.org.ar/icb2.htm (investigación y estudio argentino de los cetáceos)

http://marenostrum.org/index.htm (estudio de la biología marina)

http://www.mma.es/INTERNET/ODMMA/PN/redpn/index.htm (información oficial de la Red de Parques Nacionales de España)

http://www.rolac.unep.mx/indusamb/esp/ozono/ozono_e.htm (texto divulgativo en torno a la capa de ozono)

http://www.serviplus.com/m.ambiente/docu/esp/reco.htm (texto divulgativo en torno al aprovechamiento y reciclaje de residuos)

http://www.ecoplus.org/ (portal sobre ecología y medio ambiente)

http://www.wwwf.es/ (página web de Adena, que ofrece información sobre sus campañas)

http://www.greenpeace.es/ (web de Greenpeace, donde muestra sus principales campañas)

http://www.nodo50.org/ecologistas/ (web de Ecologistas en Acción, que ofrece noticias del medio ambiente e información sobre campañas ecologistas)

EL MUNDO EN QUE VIVIMOS

LAS RELACIONES INTERNACIONALES: LA UNIÓN EUROPEA

la adhesión *membership*
el arancel *customs tariff*
el Banco Central Europeo *European Central Bank*
la barrera de aduanas *customs barrier*
la burocracia *bureaucracy*
el ciudadano *citizen*
la colaboración *collaboration*
la Comisión Europea *European Commission*
la comunidad *community*
el Consejo de Ministros *Council of Ministers*
el Consejo Europeo *European Council*
el convenio *agreement*
la cooperación *co-operation*
el desarrollo industrial/económico *industrial/economic development*
el diputado europeo *Euro MP*
el directivo de la UE *EU directive*
eliminar las barreras *to remove barriers*
europeo *European*
la homologación *standardisation*
la integración *integration*
la libertad de circulación *freedom of movement*
la libre competencia *free competition*
el Mercado Común *Common Market*
el mercado único *single market*
la modernización *modernisation*
modernizar *to modernise*
la moneda única *single currency*
el monopolio *monopoly*
el movimiento de trabajadores *movement of workers*
las negociaciones *negotiations*
negociar *to negotiate*
el Pacto de Adhesión *Membership Pact*
los países miembros *member countries*
el Parlamento Europeo *European Parliament*
el pasaporte comunitario *Community passport*
pasar la frontera *to cross the border*
el pluralismo *pluralism*
el proteccionismo *protectionism*

el Sistema Monetario Europeo (SME) — *European Monetary System (EMS)*
la soberanía — *sovereignty*
la subvención — *subsidy*
el tratado — *treaty*
el Tribunal de Justicia Europeo — *European Court of Justice*
la unidad de cuenta europea (ECU) — *European Currency Unit (ECU)*
la unión aduanera — *customs union*
la Unión Europea — *European Union*
la zona Euro — *Eurozone*

la Política Agraria Común (PAC)	*Common Agricultural Policy (CAP)*
reforzar el sentimiento europeo	*to strengthen European feeling*
tener miedo a perder la identidad nacional	*to fear losing one´s national identity*
unión económica y monetaria	*economic and monetary union*
igualdad de oportunidades para todos los europeos	*equal opportunities for all Europeans*
aumento de las importaciones	*increase in imports*
aceptar el euro	*to accept the euro*
el Tribunal Europeo de los Derechos Humanos	*European Court of Human Rights*
la integración en Europa	*integration into Europe*
modernizar las estructuras	*to modernise structures*

La Guerra

la agresión armada — *armed aggression*
el aliado — *ally*
la alianza — *alliance*
las armas químicas — *chemical weapons*
el armisticio — *armistice*
atacar — *to attack*
el ataque — *attack*
la base — *base*
la bomba atómica — *atomic bomb*
el campo de refugiados — *refugee camp*
el cohete — *rocket*
la confrontación — *confrontation*
el criminal de guerra — *war criminal*
declarar la guerra — *to declare war*
derrotar — *to defeat*
disparar — *to fire (a gun)*
la ejecución — *execution*
el escudo humano — *human shield*
estar en guerra — *to be at war*
evacuar — *to evacuate*
las fuerzas armadas — *armed forces*
la guerra civil — *civil war*

la guerra mundial	*world war*
la guerra nuclear	*atomic warfare*
la guerra química	*chemical warfare*
una guerra sangrienta	*a bloody war*
intervenir	*to intervene*
invadir	*to invade*
la invasión	*invasion*
las maniobras	*manœuvres*
la máscara antigás	*gas mask*
el misil	*missile*
las minas antipersonales	*anti-personnel mines*
el mutilado de guerra	*disabled war veteran*
la población civil	*civil population*
perder la guerra	*to lose the war*
el prisionero de guerra	*prisoner of war*
los refugiados	*refugees*
rendirse	*to surrender*
la seguridad	*security*
torturar	*to torture*
el ultimátum	*ultimatum*
vencer	*to beat*

recurrir a la fuerza	*to resort to force*
las matanzas colectivas	*mass killings*
hubo numerosas víctimas	*there were heavy casualties*
la ruptura de una tregua	*the breaking of a truce*
aplicar sanciones económicas	*to apply economic sanctions*
el holocausto nuclear	*nuclear holocaust*
la pérdida de territorio	*loss of territory*
las relaciones diplomáticas	*diplomatic relations*
la guerra de guerrillas	*guerrilla warfare*
cometer atrocidades	*to commit atrocities*

LA PAZ

el alto al fuego	*cease-fire*
el desarme	*disarmament*
disuadir	*to deter*
disuasivo	*deterrent*
firmar la paz (con)	*to make peace (with)*
firmar un tratado	*to sign a treaty*
la iniciativa de paz	*peace initiative*
el movimiento pacifista	*peace movement*
pacificador	*peace-making*
el pacifismo	*pacifism*
la paz	*peace*
ser pacifista	*to be a pacifist*
el tiempo de paz	*peacetime*

un llamamiento al cese de hostilidades	*a call for the end of hostilities*
una manifestación pacifista	*peace demonstration/march/rally*
buscar una negociación	*to seek negotiations*
la campaña antimilitarista	*anti-military campaign*
mantener la paz	*to keep the peace*
la ayuda humanitaria	*humanitarian aid*

La Religión

adorar	*to worship*
el agnóstico	*agnostic*
Alá	*Allah*
El Corán	*Koran*
el alma *(f)*	*soul*
el ateísmo	*atheism*
el ateo	*atheist*
bendecir	*to bless*
la Biblia	*Bible*
el Budismo	*Buddhism*
el Catolicismo	*Catholicism*
el católico	*Catholic*
comulgar	*to take communion*
convertir al	*to convert to*
creer en Dios	*to believe in God*
las creyencias religiosas	*religious beliefs*
el creyente	*believer*
cristianizar	*to convert to Christianity*
el cristiano	*Christian*
la cruz	*cross*
el culto	*worship*
el cura	*priest*
el demonio	*devil*
la fe	*faith*
el Hinduísmo	*Hinduism*
el infierno	*hell*
la inmortalidad	*immortality*
ir a misa	*to go to mass*
el Islam	*Islam*
el Judaísmo	*Judaism*
el judío	*Jew, Jewish*
la mezquita	*mosque*
el milagro	*miracle*
el musulmán	*Muslim*
el obispo	*bishop*
el Papa	*Pope*
el Protestantismo	*Protestantism*
el sacerdote	*priest*
ser católico practicante	*to be a practising Catholic*
ser escéptico	*to be sceptical*
la (in)tolerancia religiosa	*religious (in)tolerance*
la vocación religiosa	*religious vocation*

practicar una religión	*to practise a religion*
los enfrentamientos religiosos	*religious confrontations*
creer en la vida despúes de la muerte	*to believe in life after death*
la infalibilidad del Papa	*the infallibility of the Pope*
convertir (a alguien) al catolicismo	*to convert (somebody) to Catholicism*
bautizar a un niño	*to baptise/christen a child*
perder la fe	*to lose one's faith*
estar en contra de mi religión	*to be against my religion*
la jerarquía eclesiástica	*ecclesiastical hierarchy*

El Tercer Mundo

el agua potable	*drinking water*
el analfabetismo	*illiteracy*
analfabeto	*illiterate*
la chabola	*shanty*
el chabolismo	*problem related to the 'chabolas'*
el control de natalidad	*birth control*
los derechos humanos	*human rights*
el desastre natural	*natural disaster*
la desesperación	*despair*
la desigualdad	*inequality*
la desnutrición	*malnutrition*
la deuda externa	*foreign debt*
empobrecerse	*to grow poorer*
la enfermedad	*disease*
la esperanza de vida	*life expectancy*
la explosión demográfica	*population explosion*
explotar	*to exploit*
la explotación infantil	*child exploitation*
la explotación sexual	*sexual exploitation*
el hambre *(f)*	*famine, hunger*
el hambre endémica	*endemic hunger*
el hundimiento económico	*economic collapse*
la industrialización	*industrialisation*
la inflación	*inflation*
la injusticia	*injustice*
la malnutrición crónica	*chronic malnutrition*
la marginación	*marginalisation*
las materias primas	*raw materials*
mendigar	*to beg*
la miseria	*misery*
morir de hambre/sed	*to die of starvation/thirst*
la mortalidad infantil	*infant mortality*
oprimido	*oppressed*
el país en vías de desarrollo	*developing country*
el país industrializado	*industrialised country*

el país subdesarrollado *underdeveloped country*
el país tercermundista *a third-world country*
el pillaje *pillage*
la planificación familiar *family planning*
la pobreza *poverty*
el régimen corrupto *corrupt regime*
la sequía *drought*
la sobreexplotación *over-exploitation*
el sufrimiento *suffering*
la superpoblación *over-population*
la supervivencia *survival*
la tasa de mortalidad *mortality rate*
el terremoto *earthquake*

las organizaciones caritativas	*charity organisations*
la alfabetización de la población	*teaching people to read and write*
vivir a expensas del Tercer Mundo	*to live at the expense of the Third World*
un niño demacrado	*an emaciated child*
tener una esperanza de vida baja	*to have a low life expectancy*
llegar a los necesitados	*to reach the needy*
depender de la caridad	*to depend on charity*
no tener recursos	*to have no resources*
reducir la deuda del Tercer Mundo	*to reduce third-world debt*
la ayuda no llega a aquéllos que la necesitan	*help does not reach those in need of it*

La Vida Urbana

el anonimato *anonymity*
aparcar *to park*
el atasco *traffic jam*
atracar *to mug*
el atraco *mugging*
el ayuntamiento *town hall, town council*
el casco urbano *city centre*
el cepo *wheelclamp*
la ciudad dormitorio *dormitory town*
el ciudadano *citizen*
estresante *stressful*
la inseguridad *insecurity*
la multa *fine*
la periferia *outskirts*
la polución *pollution*
el rascacielos *skyscraper*
los servicios públicos *public services*
el transporte público *public transport*
la vecindad *neighbourhood*
la vivienda *dwelling*
la zona peatonal *pedestrian zone*

los problemas de la zona céntrica	*inner-city problems*
la inseguridad ciudadana	*lack of safety in the streets*
la gente tiende a quedarse en casa	*people have a tendency to stay at home*
una sensación de soledad	*a feeling of loneliness*
el problema del tráfico	*the traffic problem*
ofrece muchos entretenimientos	*it has a lot to offer in terms of entertainment*
hacer las ciudades más agradables para vivir	*to make towns more pleasant to live in*

La Vida Rural

la agricultura	*agriculture*
el aire puro	*pure air*
el aislamiento	*isolation*
la calma	*calm*
el campesino	*peasant*
la caza	*hunting*
la cosecha	*harvest*
el cotilleo	*gossip*
el despoblamiento	*depopulation*
el encanto	*charm*
el éxodo rural	*drift from the land*
fértil	*fertile*
la forma de vida	*way of life*
la ganadería	*cattle breeding*
la granja	*farm*
la huerta	*market garden*
la naturaleza	*nature*
la parcela	*small plot*
la pesca	*fishing*
pintoresco	*picturesque*
el terreno	*plot*
la vida rural	*village life*

disfrutar de la paz	*to enjoy the peace*
respirar el aire puro del campo	*to breathe the pure air of the countryside*
falta de transportes públicos	*lack of public transport*
depender de un coche	*to be dependent on a car*
no hay privacidad	*there isn't any privacy*
la belleza del paisaje	*the beauty of the scenery*
tener tiempo para relacionarse con los demás	*to have time to socialise*

Cómo ampliar tu vocabulario

Cuando aprendes palabras y frases, tu memoria intenta agrupar las que van juntas, de forma que una palabra o frase te recuerde a las otras. Observa las diferentes agrupaciones que puedes hacer:

Palabras...

A ... que se refieren a un mismo tema → *enfermedad/ataque al corazón/ antiinflamatorio/vacuna*

B ... con significado similar → *filmar/rodar*

C ... con significado opuesto → *éxito/fracaso*

D ... ordenadas en forma de escalera → *letra – palabra – oración – párrafo – página – capítulo – libro*

E ... construidas partiendo de la misma palabra → *amar – enamorarse – amante – amoroso*

F ... que forman pasos dentro de un mismo proceso → *enviar un currículo – acudir a una entrevista – conseguir un trabajo*

Éstas son algunas de las formas más prácticas de formar agrupaciones. Cuando encuentres una palabra nueva, *recuerda* que relacionarla con otras ya conocidas es la mejor forma de aprenderla.

Direcciones útiles en Internet

http://europa.eu.int/ (página oficial de las instituciones de la Unión Europea)

http://www.ces.eu.int (página del Comité Económico y Social de la UE)

http://www.un.org (página de la ONU; incluye información sobre misiones de paz y de desarrollo económico)

http://www.apc.org (información sobre temas de medio ambiente, los derechos humanos, la paz, etc.)

http://www.redtercermundo.org.uy (organización que defiende los derechos de los pueblos del Tercer Mundo)

ESPAÑA

LA DICTADURA

el aislamiento — *isolation*
el Caudillo — *Spanish Fascist leader (Franco)*
el concordato — *concordat*
el cuartelazo — *military uprising*
el dictador — *dictator*
la dictadura — *dictatorship*
la época franquista — *the Franco era*
el facha — *slang term for Fascist*
la falange — *Falange (Fascist party)*
el fascismo — *Fascism*
el fascista — *Fascist*
el franquismo — *the Franco policy*
el golpe de estado — *coup d'état*
el golpismo — *tendency to military coups*
el golpista — *participant in a coup*
la guerra civil — *civil war*
el régimen — *regime*
represivo — *repressive*
totalitario — *totalitarian*

bajo el franquismo — *under Franco*
un régimen represivo — *a repressive regime*
Franco gobernó en España como dictador hasta su muerte — *Franco ruled Spain as dictator until his death*
el ostracismo internacional — *international ostracism*
la corrupción del gobierno — *government corruption*
el Tejerazo — *attempted coup by Colonel Tejero of the Civil Guard, 23 February 1981*

LA DEMOCRACIA

el abstencionismo — *abstentionism*
la administración — *administration*
la asamblea — *assembly*
la autoridad — *authority*
el boicot — *boycott*
boicotear — *to boycott*
la campaña electoral — *election campaign*
el capitalismo — *capitalism*
la circunscripción — *constituency*
el ciudadano — *citizen*
la clase alta — *upper class*
la clase baja — *lower class*

la clase media *middle class*
la clase obrera/trabajadora *working class*
la coalición *coalition*
el comunismo *communism*
comunista *communist*
el Congreso de los Diputados *the Chamber of Deputies (House of Commons)*
conservador *conservative*
la constitución *constitution*
constitucional *constitutional*
las Cortes *Spanish Parliament*
la cumbre *summit meeting*
el debate *debate*
decretar *to decree*
el decreto *decree*
el delegado *delegate*
democrático *democratic*
derechista *right-wing*
los derechos humanos *human rights*
el desacuerdo *disagreement*
la dimisión *resignation*
el diputado *MP*
el discurso *speech*
la elección general *general election*
la elección municipal *council election*
el electorado *electorate*
elegir *to elect*
el funcionario *civil servant*
gobernar *to govern*
el gobierno *government*
el grupo político *political group*
ir a las urnas *to go to the polls*
izquierdista *left-wing*
el jefe de estado *head of state*
legislar *to legislate*
legislativo *legislative*
el/la líder *leader*
el liderazgo *leadership*
manifestarse *to demonstrate*
la mayoría *majority*
la oposición *opposition*
el parlamento *parliament*
el partido *party*
el plebiscito *plebiscite*
la política *politics*
la política exterior *foreign policy*
el político *politician*
el portavoz *spokesperson*
el presidente del gobierno/primer ministro *prime minister*
el pucherazo *(inf)* *electoral fiddle*
la ratificación *ratification*
el referéndum *referendum*
la regulación *regulation*
la sesión parlamentaria *parliamentary session*
el socialismo *socialism*
socialista *socialist*
la transición a la democracia *transition to democracy*
las urnas *ballot boxes*
votar *to vote*
el voto *vote*

en mayo iremos a las urnas	*we will go to the polls in May*
hacer un llamamiento al gobierno	*to appeal to the government*
estar a favor de medidas a largo/corto plazo	*to be in favour of long-/short-term measures*
conseguir una mayoría absoluta	*to get an absolute majority*
una gran proporción de la población	*a large proportion of the population*
estar de acuerdo con la política	*to agree with the politics*
la caída del gobierno	*the downfall of the government*
una derrota aplastante	*a crushing defeat*
la ruptura de las conversaciones	*the breakdown of talks*

La Monarquía

antimonárquico *anti-monarchist*
la Casa Real *royal household*
la coronación *coronation*
la Corona Española *the Spanish Crown*
la dinastía *dynasty*
la Familia Real *royal family*
el Jefe de las Fuerzas Armadas *chief of the armed forces*
la infanta *princess*
el monarca *monarch*
monárquico *monarchist*
las obligaciones oficiales *official duties*
el palacio real *royal palace*
el prestigio *prestige*
el Príncipe de Asturias *Prince of Asturias*
el protocolo *protocol*
reinar *to reign*
los Reyes de España *King and Queen of Spain*
el soberano *sovereign*
el súbdito *subject*
tener sangre real *to have royal blood*

el príncipe heredero	*crown prince*
heredar el trono	*to inherit the crown*
renunciar al trono	*to renounce the throne*
el viaje de Estado	*state visit*
la línea de sucesión al trono	*the line of succession to the throne*
abdicar la corona	*to give up the crown*
subió al trono en 1975	*he came to the throne in 1975*

LAS AUTONOMÍAS

la autodeterminación	*self-determination*
la autonomía	*self-government*
la burocracia	*bureaucracy*
las competencias	*powers*
la Comunidad Autónoma	*self-governing region (in Spain)*
las elecciones autonómicas	*elections in a self-governing region*
Euskadi	*the Basque Country*
el euskera	*Basque (language)*
el gobierno regional	*regional government*
la lengua catalana	*the Catalan language*
la lengua gallega	*the Galician language*
la lengua vasca	*the Basque language*
el nacionalismo	*nationalism*
el País Vasco	*the Basque Country*

el derecho a la autonomía	*the right to self-government*
el separatismo vasco	*Basque separatism*
respetar la tradición	*to respect tradition*
conservar la lengua	*to preserve the language*
conservar su propia identidad	*to keep its unique identity*
las competencias transferidas a las comunidades autónomas	*the powers transferred to the autonomous regions*

UNA REGIÓN DE ESPAÑA

accidentada	*hilly*
la atmósfera	*atmosphere*
la característica	*characteristic*
el carnaval	*carnival*
concentrarse	*to be concentrated*
conmemorar	*to commemorate*
el contraste	*contrast*
cultivable	*suitable for cultivation*
el desarrollo	*development*
desprovisto de	*deprived of*
el dinamismo	*dynamism*
dotado de	*endowed with*
la economía diversificada	*varied economy*
la economía regional	*regional economy*
enorgullecerse de	*to pride itself on*
la expansión	*expansion*
famoso por	*famous for*
floreciente	*flourishing*
la imagen pública	*public image*
el litoral	*shore, coast*

llano	*flat*
medieval	*medieval*
meridional	*southern*
la mezcla	*mixture*
orgulloso de	*proud of*
el paisaje	*countryside*
el patrimonio cultural	*cultural heritage*
la pluviosidad	*average rainfall*
poblado	*populated*
promocionarse	*to promote itself*
la prosperidad	*prosperity*
retrasado	*backward*
la riqueza	*wealth*
septentrional	*northern*
sofisticado	*sophisticated*
típico	*typical*
tradicional	*traditional*
los vestigios históricos	*historical remains*
vinícola	*wine-growing*
la vitalidad	*vitality*

su situación geográfica privilegiada	*its privileged geographical position*
la suavidad de su clima	*the mildness of its climate*
la desaparición de las industrias tradicionales	*the disappearance of traditional industries*
la región se beneficia de	*the area benefits from*

DIRECCIONES ÚTILES EN INTERNET

http://www.red2000.com/spain (una guía completa sobre España por autonomías y ciudades)

http://www.meh.es/ (página del Ministerio de Economía y Hacienda)

http://www.admiweb.org (acceso a los centros oficiales y administraciones públicas españolas)

http://www.cfnavarra.es (web sobre Navarra, instituciones, servicios, etc.)

http://www.vespito.net/historia (página sobre la España del siglo XX: el franquismo, la transición, etc.)

http://www.geocities.com/CapitolHill/Lobby/8579/ (web sobre la monarquía)

http://www.fortunecity.com/victorian/cloisters/342/fresp.htm (web sobre la monarquía)

http://www.salman-psl.com/la-transicion/indexcast.html (web sobre la democracia en España)

http://www.radiovision.es/politica.htm (página web sobre los partidos políticos españoles)

CÓMO AMPLIAR TU VOCABULARIO

- Escribe en tarjetas las palabras nuevas pertenecientes a un mismo tema.
- Pon en un lado la palabra en español y en el otro la palabra inglesa correspondiente.
- Coloca las tarjetas sobre la mesa de forma que puedas ver las palabras españolas.
- Prueba a dar la traducción al inglés.
- Después, pon las tarjetas de forma que muestren las palabras en inglés e intenta decir las palabras españolas correspondientes.
- Guarda las tarjetas en una caja (clasificadas por temas) y repite el juego de cuando en cuando.
- Puedes usar pequeños ficheros para guardar las tarjetas de esta forma:

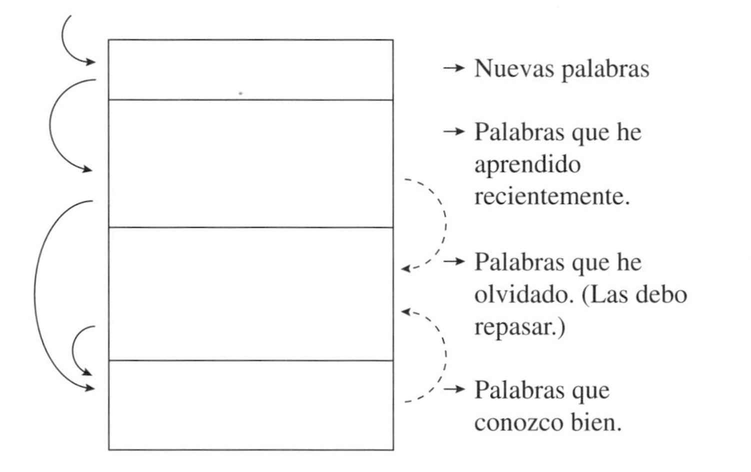

Repasa las palabras o expresiones de vez en cuando. Traslada las tarjetas de unas secciones a otras.

P.ej: Si has olvidado una palabra ya conocida, deberás colocarla en la sección de palabras olvidadas (que debes repasar) y cuando la hayas aprendido, volverá a la sección de palabras que conoces bien.

LA EXPOSICIÓN DE UN TEMA

FRASES ÚTILES PARA UNA COMPOSICIÓN

A INTRODUCCIÓN DEL TEMA

1 Deberías situar el tema dentro de un contexto:

es un problema que afecta a todas las clases sociales
it is a problem that affects all levels of society

éste es un tema que nos interesa a todos — *this is a topic that interests all of us*

este tema provoca mucha controversia — *this question causes a lot of controversy*

la importancia de este problema no puede ser subestimada
the importance of this problem cannot be overstated/underestimated

éste no es un problema nuevo — *this is not a new problem*

el problema ha alcanzado tales proporciones que…
the problem has reached such proportions that …

este problema es mucho más serio de lo que la gente piensa
this problem is much more serious than people think

2 También deberías indicar en la introducción qué es lo que vas a exponer:

vamos a examinar los argumentos a favor y en contra
let us examine the arguments for and against

trataré de determinar las causas principales de…
I shall try to determine the main causes of …

mi objetivo principal es… — *my main aim is …*

veamos las ventajas y los inconvenientes
let us see the advantages and the disadvantages

vamos a abordar el aspecto de... — *let us tackle the aspect of...*

para tener una visión más clara de la situación — *to have a clearer picture of the situation*

El Desarrollo Del Argumento

1 Puedes empezar un párrafo con una pregunta retórica:

¿es posible generalizar? *is it possible to generalise?*

¿cómo podemos, entonces, tratar el problema de… ? *how then shall we deal with the problem of… ?*

¿es el problema tan grave como parece? *is the problem as serious as it seems?*

¿podemos decir que… ? *can we say that… ?*

2 Otras frases para empezar un párrafo incluirían:

para comenzar, sería útil… *to start off, it would be useful to…*

vamos a considerar, en primer lugar,… *let us first consider…*

para profundizar en el tema *to go into the matter in more depth*

a primera vista *at first sight*

en primer/segundo/tercer lugar *in the first/second/third place*

para empezar, examinemos… *to start off with, let us examine…*

otro aspecto del problema es… *another side of the problem is…*

vamos a abordar otro aspecto *let us tackle another aspect*

3 Cuando quieras establecer un hecho o certeza puedes utilizar frases como:

no cabe duda de que… *there's no room for doubt that…*

no se puede negar que… *one can't deny that…*

parece ser que… *it seems that…*

lo que es cierto es que… *what is certain is that…*

se calcula que… *it is estimated that ...*

es indudable que… *there is no doubt that ...*

la verdad es que… *the fact of the matter is that ...*

el factor más importante es que… *the most important factor is that ...*

como todo el mundo sabe *as everyone knows*

un 50% de los entrevistados opinaron que… *fifty per cent of those interviewed considered that…*

según algunos estudios	*according to some studies*
durante los últimos años	*during recent years*
se ha dicho que…	*it has been claimed that…*
es sabido que…	*it's known that…*
es claro que…	*it's clear that…*
es verdad que…	*it's true that…*
de acuerdo con una investigación	*according to an investigation*
actualmente se calcula que…	*at the moment it is estimated that…*

4 Para expresar tus opiniones o las de otros:

es escandaloso…	*it is scandalous to…*
sería una locura…	*it would be madness to…*
uno debe ponerse en contra de…	*one must object to…*
es intolerable que…	*it's intolerable that…*
me parece lógico que…	*it seems logical to me that…*
me preocupa que…	*I am worried that…*
a mi parecer	*in my opinion*
personalmente	*personally*
a mi modo de ver	*in my view*
mucha gente piensa que…	*many people think that…*
ésta no es una opinión que yo comparta	*this is not an opinion I share*
no estoy ni a favor ni en contra de esto	*I am neither for nor against it*
no estoy totalmente a favor de…	*I am not entirely in favour of…*
eso sería demasiado optimista	*that would be too optimistic*
estoy a favor de…	*I am in favour of…*
estoy en contra de…	*I am against…*
a nadie le importa si…	*nobody cares whether…*
es de extremada importancia que…	*it is of extreme importance that…*
parece mentira que…	*it seems incredible that…*
es inadmisible que…	*it's unacceptable that…*
es lamentable que…	*it is to be regretted that…*

es inútil ...	*there's no point in ...*
es difícil de imaginar que ...	*it's hard to imagine that ...*
es inconcebible que ...	*it's inconceivable that ...*
es vergonzoso que ...	*it's disgraceful that ...*
no me sorprende que ...	*I am not surprised that ...*
la sociedad no puede tolerar ...	*society cannot tolerate ...*

5 Cualquiera que sean tus opiniones, deberías mostrar las opiniones contrarias:

por otra parte	*on the other hand*
examinemos la otra cara de la moneda	*let us examine the other side of the coin*
por otro lado, algunos afirman que ...	*on the other hand, some maintain that ...*
otro hecho que debería mencionar es ...	*another fact that I should mention is ...*
otro lado del problema es ...	*another side of the problem is ...*
las opiniones están divididas	*opinions are divided*

CONCLUSIÓN

Al final de tu exposición necesitas resumir lo expuesto y llegar a una conclusión:

todo parece indicar que ...	*everything seems to point to the fact that ...*
de esto se deduce que ...	*it follows from this that ...*
uno podría bien preguntarse si ...	*one might well wonder whether ...*
en definitiva	*when all the arguments have been heard*
teniendo en cuenta todos los puntos de vista	*taking into account all points of view*
para resumir	*to sum up*
concluyendo	*in conclusion*

EXPRESIONES COLOQUIALES

aguar la fiesta	*to be a wet blanket*
armar una bronca	*to start a fight*
cantarle las cuarenta (a alguien)	*to tell someone off*
dar la lata	*to make a nuisance of oneself*
dormir a pierna suelta	*to sleep like a log*
echar chispas	*to be hopping mad*
echar indirectas	*to make insinuations*
echar un trago	*to have a drink*
echar una cana al aire	*to have a little fling*
echar una ojeada a	*to glance at*
estar en las nubes	*to be day-dreaming*
estar hasta la coronilla (de)	*to be fed up (with)*
estar hecho un asco	*to be filthy*
estar sin blanca	*to be flat broke*
estirar la pata	*to kick the bucket*
faltarle un tornillo (a alguien)	*to have a screw loose*
hablar por los codos	*to talk one's head off*
hacer buenas migas	*to get along well*
hacer el ridículo	*to make a fool of oneself*
hacerse el sueco	*to pretend not to understand*
llevarse un chasco	*to have a disappointment*
llover a cántaros	*to rain cats and dogs*
meter las narices en todo	*to poke one's nose into everything*
no entender ni papa	*not to understand a thing*
no importar un bledo	*not to give a damn about it*
pedir peras al olmo	*to expect the impossible*
ser un viejo verde	*to be a dirty old man*
tener mal genio	*to be bad-tempered*
tener malas pulgas	*to be short-tempered*
tomarle el pelo (a alguien)	*to pull someone's leg*

LOS VERBOS Y EL INFINITIVO

Algunos verbos pueden ir seguidos de otro verbo en infinitivo. Unas veces el infinitivo sigue directamente al verbo y otras necesita preposiciones como: **a, de, con, en, por** y **para.**

Ej: Amenazó con denunciarme. *He threatened to report me.*
¿Quieres dejar de moverte? *Will you stop moving?*

El estudiante de lengua española encuentra muchas veces difícil el uso correcto de las preposiciones. Por ello, a continuación se incluye una lista de los verbos más comunes que pueden ir seguidos del infinitivo (con o sin preposición).

A Verbos que van seguidos directamente de un infinitivo:

aconsejar	*to advise to*
acordar	*to agree to*
anhelar	*to long to*
apetecer	*to feel like (doing)*
confesar	*to confess to*
conseguir	*to manage to*
creer	*to believe*
deber	*to have to/must/ought*
decidir	*to decide to*
dejar	*to let/to allow to*
desear	*to want/to wish to*
elegir	*to chose to*
esperar	*to hope/to expect to*
evitar	*to avoid (doing)*
fingir	*to pretend to*
hacer	*to make*
imaginar	*to imagine (doing)*
intentar	*to try to*
jurar	*to swear to*
lograr	*to manage to/to succeed in*
mandar	*to order to*
necesitar	*to need to*
negar	*to deny*
odiar	*to hate (doing)*
ofrecer	*to offer to*
oír	*to hear (doing)*
olvidar	*to forget to*
ordenar	*to order to*
parecer	*to seem to*
pedir	*to ask to*
pensar	*to intend to/to plan to*
permitir	*to allow to*
planear	*to plan to*
poder	*to be able to*
preferir	*to prefer to*
pretender	*to try to*
procurar	*to try hard to*
prohibir	*to forbid ... to*
prometer	*to promise to*
proponer	*to suggest (doing)*

querer	*to want to*
recordar	*to remember to*
rehusar	*to refuse to*
resolver	*to resolve to*
saber	*to know how to*
sentir	*to be sorry to*
soler	*to be accustomed to*
temer	*to fear to*
ver	*to see (doing)*

B Los siguientes verbos van seguidos de 'a' + infinitivo:

acertar a	*to manage to*
acostumbrarse a	*to be used to (doing)*
aficionarse a	*to grow fond of (doing)*
animar a	*to encourage to*
aprender a	*to learn to*
apresurarse a	*to hurry to*
atreverse a	*to dare to*
ayudar a	*to help to*
comenzar a	*to begin to*
comprometerse a	*to undertake to*
conducir a	*to lead to*
contribuir a	*to contribute to*
decidirse a	*to decide to/to make up one's mind to*
dedicarse a	*to devote oneself to*
desafiar a	*to challenge ... to*
disponerse a	*to get ready to*
echarse a	*to begin to*
empezar a	*to begin to*
enseñar a	*to teach to*
esperar a	*to wait until*
forzar a	*to force to*
impulsar a	*to urge to*
incitar a	*to incite to*
inclinar a	*to incline to*
invitar a	*to invite to*
ir a	*to be going to*
llegar a	*to manage to*
llevar a	*to lead to*
mandar a	*to send to*
meterse a	*to begin to*
negarse a	*to refuse to*
obligar a	*to oblige to*
oponerse a	*to be opposed to (doing)*
pasar a	*to go on to*
ponerse a	*to begin to*
precipitarse a	*to rush to*
prepararse a	*to get ready to*
probar a	*to try to*
resignarse a	*to resign oneself to*
resistirse a	*to resist*
romper a	*to start (suddenly) to*
tender a	*to tend to*
volver a	*to do (something) again*

C Los siguientes verbos van seguidos de 'de' + infinitivo:

aburrirse de	*to get bored with (doing)*
acabar de	*to have just*
acordarse de	*to remember*
acusar de	*to accuse of*
alegrarse de	*to be pleased to*
asombrarse de	*to be surprised at (doing)*

avergonzarse de	*to be ashamed of*
cansarse de	*to tire of*
cesar de	*to stop (doing)*
cuidar de	*to take care to*
deber de	*to have to/must (supposition)*
dejar de	*to stop (doing)*
disuadir de	*to dissuade from*
encargarse de	*to take charge of*
guardarse de	*to take care not to*
haber de	*to have to*
hartarse de	*to be fed up with*
jactarse de	*to boast of*
olvidarse de	*to forget to*
parar de	*to stop (doing)*
pasar de *(inf)*	*to be uninterested in (doing)*
presumir de	*to boast about (doing)*
terminar de	*to stop (doing)*
tratar de	*to try to*

D Los verbos siguientes van seguidos de 'en', 'por', 'con' y 'para' + infinitivo:

acabar por	*to end up (doing)*
amenazar con	*to threaten with*
consentir en	*to consent to*
consistir en	*to consist of (doing)*
convenir en	*to agree to*
dudar en	*to hesitate to*
empezar por	*to begin by (doing)*
esforzarse en/por	*to struggle to*
hacer bien en	*to be right to*
hacer mal en	*to be wrong to*
insistir en	*to insist on*
interesarse en	*to be interested in*
luchar por	*to struggle for*
optar por	*to opt for*
pensar en	*to think of (doing)*
persistir en	*to persist in*
quedar en	*to agree to*
tardar en	*to take a long time (doing)*